THE LIFE OF
SHIRŌ MIYAZAKI

An Itinerant Artist of the 1930s
Through His Letters

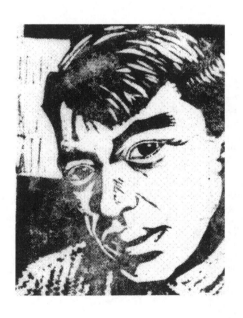

Order this book online at www.trafford.com
or email orders@trafford.com

Most Trafford titles are also available at major online book retailers.

Printed in the United States of America.

ISBN: 978-1-4269-7948-4 (sc)
ISBN: 978-1-4269-7949-1 (e)

Library of Congress Control Number: 2011912392

Trafford rev. 01/11/2012

 www.trafford.com

North America & international
toll-free: 1 888 232 4444 (USA & Canada)
phone: 250 383 6864 ♦ fax: 812 355 4082

DEDICATIONS

This book is dedicated to the following five persons with gratitude from the bottom of my heart.

First and foremost, to the memory of my brother, Shirō Miyazaki, a struggling artist who endeavored to become great but couldn't beat the odds that were stacked against him and died at the young age of 30. Had he not written these letters, this book would not have been possible.

George Tsutakawa, Shirō's loyal and true friend and buddy, to whom he was able to open up his mind and heart, keeper of his artworks and letters.

Dr. William Gamble, whose critique of Shirō's art encouraged him to continue his work and for storing his art and letters during World War II.

Mary Ikeda Shigaya, life long friend,who by her conversation with Ayame, George Tsutakawa's wife, made it possible for me to obtain my brother's art and letters and to give them back to the world.

Grace Arimura, dear friend, who forever keeping after me to publish this book.

Forward

In the summer of 1992, an old friend in Seattle, Mary Shigaya, called to tell me of an event that had happened to her recently. My friend who was a teacher of Ikebana, the art of Japanese flower arrangement, was traveling by car with a fellow teacher to a flower show. During the trip, Mary was telling her friend of the Japanese families that used to live in her neighborhood in Seattle back in the 1930s. One of the names she mentioned was Miyazaki. Her friend wondered out loud, "I wonder if they were related to Shirō Miyazaki". Mary said, "Yes, in fact we visited Shirō's brother last year in Illinois". Her friend told her that her husband had been trying to locate Shirō's relatives for years without success. Her husband was the renown artist and water fountain sculptor, George Tsutakawa, professor emeritus of fine arts at University of Washington. She said that George had kept my brother's art from before the war and was thinking of having a one last exhibit for him and dispose of my brother's works as George was getting along in years. My brother had died in 1940.

Taking up Mary's suggestion, I called George and he was happy to find a kin after all these years. He asked if we were going to be in the Seattle area in the near future and I told him that we were going to a wedding in Los Angeles in August and could stop by on the way.

I remembered George since he used to visit his uncle who lived just four houses away from us and I used to played with one of his cousins who was of my age. Of course, he probably didn't remember me except possibly as Shirō's little kid brother, Shirō being fifteen years my senior.

When we visited George at his lovely home atop the hill overlooking beautiful Lake Washington, he took us up to his attic where he had stored Shirō's artwork. He told me that Shirō had bold strokes and believed that he could have become a great artist had he not died at such a young age. George said that he wanted to keep just one painting and that he would send me the rest. He also gave me all of Shirō's linoleum blocks including an uncut unfinished block of an Oklahoman migrant family standing by their broken down jalopy, next to a billboard touting, "Next time try the train".

Also included was a bundle of letters Shirō had written to George and Dr. Bill Gamble[1] while in California. Since I was only six when he left for California and fourteen when he died, Shirō was practically a stranger to me; therefore, when I read his heart rendering letters, it was then I first realized the hardship he had to endure pursuing his love for art.

The letters and postcards in this book were written by Shirō to his dear friends and artists George Tsutakawa and Dr. William Gamble, both living in Seattle when the letters were written. Shirō's letters to George were all in Japanese and I have translated them the best I could. I was surprised at his command of the Japanese language. It must have come from his love to read and a sharp mind. He knew many Japanese phrases and kanji characters I never knew or even heard before, though I somehow had graduated from a Japanese university. Using two kanji (Chinese character) dictionaries, two Japanese language dictionaries and two Japanese-English dictionaries, I still had trouble and still doubt that I was able to grasp his thoughts adequately. Kanji phrases are difficult if you don't know its pronunciation and/or meaning. Frequently, two or more kanji characters are combined to make a word that has an altogether different meaning than the meanings of the two individual characters added together. When I didn't know it's meaning, and couldn't find the combined characters in the kanji dictionaries; after determining its pronunciation, I first looked it up in the Japanese-English dictionary. If it was not in there, then I tried my luck with the Japanese language dictionary. If I still couldn't find it, then I took the meaning of each character from the Jigen Chinese Character dictionary and tried to combine them and come up with a meaning that made some sort of sense with the rest of the text. Many times, I used a direct translation in order to be as close to the phrases as he wrote them so the reader could look into his poetic mind, rather than using a more generalized term. (e.g. 'footsteps of the rain' as he said it, rather than 'the pitter patter of the raindrops'.) Some Japanese words or phrases, I left in Japanese, especially in his poems, and put the English translation in brackets [ ].adjacent to them.

The letters from Shirō to Dr. Gamble were all in English so I copied exactly as he wrote them. His spelling and punctuations were not changed in order to convey his command of English or lack thereof. It also gives the letters another flavor beyond his quaint descriptions and phrases. I first

---

1   See Introduction page for Dr.Gamble.

started to add "(sic)" after each misspelled word to denote that it is not a typographical error but finally decided against it, since the reader should have little difficulty in deciphering the misspelled words or the intent of the sentence.

As background information, I have also included as Appendices, some correspondences of my father's that George had, which were written to him and to Shirō. Also included is father's so-called Will. It sounds more like the Ten Commandments and was written to our mother when he first set sail alone for America in 1915. Also included are translated excerpts of eulogies written in a San Francisco Japanese Language newspaper's memorial edition following Shirō's death.

Anything in brackets [ ] are my personal comments or interpretations and are not a part of Shirō's letters.

In reading Shirō's Japanese letters to George, you may notice that the date of the letter and/or the recipient's name are at the end of the letter. This is the common practice in Japanese letter writing.

In Japanese words, places and names, wherever long vowels are used, I have used the characters, ā, ē, ī, ō and ū. This is because there are many words that are written the same except for the vowel being either short or long. (e.g. the surname Satō with a short 'o' could mean sugar or village. I have a friend who's last name is Nōmi. However, nomi is a flea so one has to be careful.

Also in Japanese, each vowel is pronounced only one way. A is always pronounced as the first A in away. E is always pronounced like the first E in ever. I is always pronounced like the I in Italy. O is always pronounces like the O in Oklahoma and U is always pronounced like the O in woman or woo, not the U in ugh or ugly. Now pronounce the car, Honda. It's not Handa as you always hear in the television commercials. Handa, incidentally is also a surname just like Honda.

Shū Miyazaki

INTRODUCTION

A short introduction delving into the family history is necessary to better understand Shirō's tumultuous life.

Our father, Hideo, was born on July 24, 1888, in a small fishing village of Tsubaki-domari in Tokushima prefecture on the island of Shikoku, Japan. During the last year of middle school[2] (equivalent to our 11th grade), he applied and was accepted to both the Army and Naval Academies but chose the Army. Illness cut short his military career and he became an elementary school teacher in Kōbe.

Our mother, Kuni, was born on September 10, 1889 and raised in the city of Gojō in Nara prefecture. Her father was a fairly well-to-do merchant who owned a kimono store. I don't know how the two met, but according to my stepmother, they met when they were both patients in the same hospital. When they married, he was taken in to our mother's Shimamoto family as a yōshi (adopted son); however, he planned eventually to leave the clan and set up his own lineage with the Miyazaki name.

Convinced that there was no future for him in Japan, he decided to seek his fortune in America. Leaving his wife and five year old Shirō, he arrived alone in Seattle in 1915. He worked at the elite Rainier Club as a schoolboy while learning English. Later he worked on a railroad gang laying rails for the Great Northern and/or Northern Pacific RR and in Alaska at a whale oil rendering factory. In the early 1920s, he started his own exporting business in Seattle, shipping lumber to Japan. The great Kanto earthquake of 1923 worked in his favor as lumber was greatly needed to rebuild Tōkyō and Yokohama. He then landed a job as a special correspondent for one of Japan's largest newspaper, the Osaka Mainichi , covering the Pacific Northwest. At the same time, to augment his income,

---

2   Middle School (chūgakkō) in Japan was from grades 7 through 11 until after WW II when General MacArthur changed the school system from the 6-5-3-3 to the present 6-3-3-4 system and middle schools then became grades 7 through 9. Middle school was not compulsory and required an entrance exam. Those not accepted usually went on to a three-year 'higher elementary school' (kōtō-shōgakkō).

he also became a life insurance agent for Sun Life Assurance Company of Canada, selling life insurance to Japanese immigrants, covering an area as far away as Central Oregon.

Shirō was born in Gojō on May 24th, 1910 and lived with our mother at her parent's home. In 1920, our father called our mother to join him in Seattle but decided that Shirō should get a Japanese education, so he was left in the care of his maternal grandparents and uncle. Being left alone in Japan without his parents, Shirō became a problem child and once left home and could not be found for several days. I believe he graduated middle school. I don't know how much English he learned in middle school, but does write in one of his letters (Letter #45) that English was his weak point and got only Es and Fs. He arrived in the United States in 1929, went to Garfield High School in Seattle and graduated in 1932. The feud between Shirō and our father was well known within the Japanese community and is evident in the letter from father to son written in 1940 (See Appendix IV). Both being hard headed with neither side giving in, the father disowned and kicked Shirō out of the house after graduation, whereupon he left for California to seek his fortune. This is where his letters begin.

Shirō and George Tsutakawa's friendship started when they both won awards in a national art contest, sponsored by Scholastic Magazine in 1932, in the linoleum cut print division. George won first prize and Shirō an honorable mention. According to George, they first met at a photo session honoring Seattle's student winners. They soon became fast friends because of their mutual interest in art and as they both spoke Japanese better than English. George was born in Seattle, the same year as Shirō but was sent to Japan in 1917 and lived with his maternal grandmother until 1927 when he returned to the States. After graduating Broadway High School in 1932, he went on to study art at the University of Washington and later became a professor of fine arts there, retiring in 1983 and died in December 1997. He was especially renown throughout the world for his water fountain sculptures, some of which can be found at the National Cathedral in Washington D.C., the Ala Moana Mall in Honolulu, in Indianapolis, Indiana, Anaheim and Fresno in California, as well as several in Japan. For the life and work of George Tsutakawa, read "George Tsutakawa" by Martha Kingsbury, © 1990 by the Bellvue Art Museum (ISBN 0-295-97020-0).

Shirō's friendship with Bill Gamble started in 1934 when George Tsutakawa asked him to critique one of Shirō's linoleum block prints. They met each other only once when Shirō returned to Seattle to attend our mother's funeral in 1937. Dr. Gamble also graduated University of Washington and later became a professor of fine arts at Michigan State University with two doctorates, in fine arts and in art education. He retired and lived in East Lansing, Michigan until his death in 2009. My wife and I were fortunate enough to locate and visit with him in 1995.

As you will find in his letters, Shirō led a nomadic life moving from one farm to the next throughout the San Joaquin Valley during the growing seasons and then to San Francisco or Los Angeles during the winter months to work at whatever job he could find, yet continuing his art studies. Being constantly poor and living among the poor, he became a fellow traveler and joined the Communist Party but later wrote that he had quit the party. Since he could not keep his works with him as he was moving around so frequently, he asked George to keep them for him. During the war after President FDR signed the infamous Executive Order 9066, that authorized rounding up all Japanese American living along the Pacific Coast to placing them in concentration camps (FDR's words) built in the remote and desolate areas of our great country, but generally referred to as 'Relocation Centers', Bill Gamble stored all of the art works George had as well as those of some other Japanese American artists, ,in his garage for the duration of the war.

After our mother died in 1937, our father returned to Japan taking my sister and me with him in the spring of 1940. I returned to the US in 1953. My only regret is that I never had the chance to get to know my brother. I am, however, eternally grateful to George and Bill for saving his art works and correspondences, that I was able to see his art works and though his letters, get to know of his accomplishments and the sad and cruel life he had to endure.

Shirō at 6 months

Shirō 2 years old

**Shirō 5 years old with parents
(July 1915)**

Shirō at age 15

Shirō (19) with sister (6) and Brother (3)
(Seattle August 1929)

Contents

Appendices

LETTER #1

From Shirō to Undisclosed Friends

Greetings to all,

I haven't written for some time. What has happened to me since, is all written in my letter to Geo. so please read that.

The candies I received from you when I left, were so good we cleaned them all up. I'm not asking you to send me more but aren't candies wonderful? I bought a five-pound box of Kisses and have it in my room. I don't know who invented milk chocolate but I always think of him as an admirable guy.

Is there anyone who'll buy my art? The pay is so low I think of such things.

Take care of yourselves and I'll write again.

Shiro

[No date is on the letter but George Tsutakawa has marked on it 10-15-1932

The mailing address was Rte 3 Box 228, Visalia, California.]

Letter #2

From Shirō to George Tsutakawa

A Letter to George

Shirō Miyazaki

Introduction

I always think I would like to write an artistic letter without disgracing my conscience. To me, because a letter is a type of literature, it is art. In fact, it is a special type of art. A letter can exist only between individuals who don't have society as an object. It's talk between an individual and another individual. Therefore, a letter will most likely not ramble on without end, similar to an individual's daily conversation; however, rather than a letter read only once, when a letter is treated as a piece of art, it has to have that something that is common with poem, novel, painting, music, etc. That something, which is common with a piece of art, is the artistic effort to illustrate better with a comfortable rhythmic flow. The effort, research and phrasing needed for a complete expression always requires time. I'm not intentionally lazy, but this is the reason my letter was late. That's how it was.

Main Discourse

Chapter 1 - Report

Shiro arrived safely. He's working every day while eating grapes. End of report.

2

Chapter 2 - Blue Skies

The black rails of the railroad, the highway and the forest of telephone poles are twisted into a single rope and become one great artery that connects cities to cities of concrete blocks piled on top of black smoke.

The artery does not differentiate between day and night but is life itself. Our bus proceeds on this highway just like fresh red corpuscles boiling and flowing as they leap forth from the heart.

This highway traverses along the Cascade Range. A range of manly and saintly mountains, mountain after mountain. The thick asphalt covered road, full of elasticity, stretched far south through hills and valleys. The blueness of the sky soaks in and stings the eyes caused by lack of sleep. The sky too, starts to brighten like the light of a southern country. Cows are licking the yellow hill that has been mown of hay. A flock of turkey is pecking through a wheat field on the hillside that has been reaped. Through the middle of this yellow field, blue skies and white clouds, the black highway stretches southward. The road starts up a slight incline, winding like the back of a top shell when suddenly, passing though some boulders, we're flying skyward several thousand feet up a steep ravine. Then we're looking down on a bounteous mountain stream with green banks, whose source must be at some distant mountain glacier.

After following it down to the valley below, we start to climb again. Each time we do this, my ears ring and the eardrums pop in and out. I become uneasy, thinking that if we climb any higher, my eardrums would balloon out like a bubble gum and burst! Remember when we went fishing in Alaska and the air sacs popped out of those fishes we pulled up from the deep blue sea? That was caused by the change in pressure. Going up and down, I tired of the yellow scenery.

Closing my eyes, I thought of the book I recently read, "The Life of a KOPF" (see footnote 1) and continued thinking about my paintings and myself. As the contradictions of capitalism becomes more piercing and violent, and even with the authorities' piercing, violent suppression after suppression, the countless beaten down young KOPFs keep rising. I compared my current worthlessness to their burning with hope. Today, as an interesting time (see footnote 2) begins, I no longer have any taste for it.

In this time of change, what can I accomplish with my art? Is it only at this worthlessness that my broken down spirit is gazing upon, without feeling for a miserable solution and for myself? Leaving home with books on my back, isn't this the time to make a desperate resolution to myself that I will not return even if I'm dying and without a trade? Yet, I feel nothing. My feelings have died. Like an unturned playing card, I let myself float and flow with the tide of destiny and whether I can get a trade or not, it's hard for me to return to that town. Without this sorrow, I may have been able to chew off more of my father's brain.

Without knowing it, the highway has slid into a red layer of dirt. Oh, the beauty of the contrast between the red dirt, the black highway and the blue sky!

(Footnote 1) KOPF is the abbreviation of the Japanese Proletariat Culture Federation.

(Footnote 2) "Interesting time" --- a phrase from Sakamoto Ryoma's[3] letter which read: "As the country's state of affairs becomes more acute day by day, it has become a very interesting time and we can now enjoy it". I don't mean here that an imperialistic war is imminent but the destruction of capitalism's fortification.

Chapter 3 - The Smell and the Fragrance of the Streets

Shiro arrived in Oakland. I was awakened by Tanaka's voice who was sitting next to me. He had covered my lap with a warm blanket. Outside was pitch black. Suddenly it lit up as the bus slid onto a ferryboat. "Twenty minutes to San Francisco", called the bus driver as he opened the door. Thinking to myself, "Well, well. I wonder what San Francisco is like". I stepped out onto the deck. To the starboard, a searchlight's strong ray flowed out from Goat Island. On the port side I could see the lights of fifteen or so of what looked like warships. Will these ships start a miserable tornado of a sea battle with shelling, explosions, screams and cries? The streetlights of San Francisco shine sleepily beyond the eyelids of the night fog. In the dining room, about a dozen men and women who appear to be

---

3   Ryoma Sakamoto was a noted young samurai during the Meiji Restoration Era.]

Nisei are noisily drinking coffee. The night wind from the Pacific Ocean through the Golden Gate is chilly.

This boat without any bow or stern docked easily. Like fishes being released from a bucket to the sea, the car leaped energetically onto the asphalt again and run straight through between the square buildings. The bus makes a turn into an alley and then into a garage when the announcement comes "San Francisco, twenty minute rest".

"Goodbye." The bus carrying Tanaka-san and Mura-san turns the corner and disappears. Left in the empty steel reinforced concrete garage, it was 2:30 AM as we made our way out to find the Japanese town. There were still a number of people wandering the streets. Half of them were U.S. navy men, shouldering the burden of the strongest country in the world and with alcohol on their breath. Walking two or three hours, up and down the hills on the hard pavement, our feet began to hurt. Dawn broke. People became scarce. The bars(?) are sweeping out the revelers.

Got our lodging. Empty handed and deciding to see the town, we got on a streetcar going to Golden Gate Park. Ding, ding, dong. The dark green leaves of the Sago palm drooped heavily. Out the window, no matter how far we go, there is nothing green. The streets are without grass or trees and are empty, pale and lifeless. The only thing filling this emptiness is the smell of the gutter.

Is this how the town is? This town, where I plan to start a new life, felt like a dry, dry dump. Wherever I looked, were rows of wooden 4 to 5 storied old fashion apartment buildings. The rear rooms on the top floor probably rent for about five dollars a month. To start a reckless life in such a place like this should be interesting. I don't mind spending a little more renting a room in a house that has a yard and trees, but like my love life, it's seems to be an impossible wish. The September sun, with an indifferent tired feeling, mixes with the smell of the gutter.

It's a separate heaven! Getting off at the end of the line and walking on the grass along a brick-laden road, bushes, large trees, giant trees grow closely together and drip with greenery. After looking at the darkened yellow sidewalks and buildings, I stared in wonder at the fresh greenness of this park. Yet, I didn't feel I had the time or was in the frame of mind to sit down and take in this entire splendor. Please let me remember it.

We came to sightsee and even as in the olden days of Yajikita[4], sightseeing is still rough and bustling.

After smelling the fragrant tropical orchids in the botanical garden, we entered the art museum. It's splendid with its lighting and size! With paintings from Renaissance to Modern, I thought, "How unfortunate Sadao couldn't see this before he returned to Japan". One of my favorite, Henry Poe's[?] landscape painting was there. I couldn't help being amazed that there are so many famous sculptures and reliefs, originals and copies, from ancient Greece to the present. "I'm going to come here and study", I thought to myself as I looked at an exhibit of primitive art. Why? Because I saw some two thousand year old potteries with pictures, that one might think Piccasso might have copied. A Japanese art section had Uchikake [a long outer garment], palanquin, stone lanterns and Tsurikane [a hanging gong], as well as an armored samurai doll that looked so real whether from near or afar.

There was a room of only watches and clocks. After I went between countless pieces of art with the fragrance of European roses, I came to a place with a number of exhibits. I became frightened while looking at one woman designer's individual exhibit. It felt as if a lot of great athletes were in front waiting for me. The picture you painted two or three years ago of Hoshi-san leaping and my block print of a gas tank was hanging on the wall in one room. They were mixed in with some Japanese American high school exhibit and though there were some good artists, I didn't feel intimidated. About a third of this museum is full of weapons but since I didn't have enough time, I went to one room and standing in the middle like a lighthouse, made one complete revolution and left.

On a bench by the bandstand, two or three guys were eating in the shade. In the aquarium, seeing over twenty species of trout, from small minnow like Yellowstone trout to jack trout about the size of a bonito was impressive. After seeing the sights of this park, soaking in the midday sun and covered with dust, I hurried to the exit when a squirrel came and bowed as if to ask for something but the only thing I had was an empty stomach.

---

4   Yajikita is short for Yajiro & Kitahachi, two fabled happy go lucky bumbling travelers.

Since we paid twenty-five cents this morning, we can ride the streetcar all day (on Sundays it's 24 hours from 5 AM). After eating some domburi [rice bowl], we got on the streetcar again and went to see Seal Rock. Seal Rock is a black boulder in the Pacific Ocean not far from shore and is all white with sea gulls. The ocean waves are powerful indeed. The summer sea of my homeland is calling me.

"The seals have returned from their summer vacation together with their children. Look till your heart's content. It's only ten cents!" This is probably what the man by the telescope is saying, but he speaks too fast for me to understand. Nobody looked, nor did we. From the cliff below the observation deck, the wide sandy beach stretches south beyond the summer fog. The waves, full of elasticity, keep on rising then crumbling with a swoosh at an angle onto the sand, then flow rapidly back out to the sea, leaving the white sea shells to roll and sparkle. Again with a shoosh, the collapsing waves return. These waves! This sun! In the middle of summer, I want to go swimming in the nude.

The road by the seashore is buried with a flood of black roofed cars. On top of that, the various curves of the playground move around with complicated speed.

Chapter 4 - The Valley

Visalia is about ten hour's ride by bus from San Francisco and lies in the southeastern part of the Sacramento Valley. It's a fairly large town ranging from fifty to sixty steel reinforced concrete buildings to hotels built of wood whose windows seem ready to fall off. Actually, there's not a single factory and the town relies solely on the farmers. Therefore, as the waves of rural panic deepen year by year, the town becomes impoverished along with the farms. George, as you were born and raised here, you may recollect and say, "This area has declined from the time I was here." The hotel lady, who caters to farm laborers, laments with that peculiar smile Japanese have when things go wrong and are sad, "In hard times like this, nobody comes to town and it's really lonesome. Under these conditions, we won't be able to continue any more".

I hate this kind of town where the townspeople, without any productivity, look down on farmers, overcharge them and with that money live in better homes, wear better clothes, eat better food. To top it off, they even have better recreation and stay at high price places. So, I'm going to walk out of this town.

The day after I arrived here, we walked the country road for about 14 miles to the home of George's uncle. The fields are flat, made up of orchards or yellowish brown grassland with horses standing idly by. They say it rains in the winter and spring, but looking at it, I can't believe it rains at all during the whole year. The river looks more like a shallow ditch with a little water and the mica in the dried sand on the banks and roadside sparkle in the sun light like gold dust. Although it's the latter part of September and it may sound strange to call it mid-summer, the sweat won't evaporate even while resting in the shade. It's the kind of heat that reminds me of the sound of cicadas.

The orchards are well made. Water is pumped up by electric pump. It's because water is available around here if you dig down fifty or a hundred feet. They say that further south, they have to go down as far as five hundred to a thousand feet; however, pumping it out day after day, they say the water table drops about two feet per year.

Fruits in short, there are any kind of fruit. Peaches, persimmons, oranges, lemons, grapes, figs, watermelon, pomegranates, prunes, olives, etc. are all lined up along both sides of the road. The tastiest are the grapes. Among them, the seedless Thompson, which is in season now, is the best. All things have their time but the best is when they are in season. Of course, we can't stand the mosquitoes when they are in season, but even there, I read in a book of haiku, that there is a flavor in the first mosquito. By the roadside, giant sunflowers are in full bloom. Looking at any flower, any petal, they show the strength of the summer sun itself that pleasantly moves my artistic feeling like a breeze.

Walking four hours under the scorching sun, we finally reached our destination.

"Hello!" "Oh! Did you walk here? If you had asked in town, anybody would have brought you here."

Then after fourteen years, the conversation between uncle and nephews began. In the middle of this field, the uncle has a fifty to sixty acre vineyard and lives a widower's life alone in a barn-like single storied house.

8

The floor is rough as if the wind had eroded it. For furniture, there was a bed with springs, three beds like the ones we slept in Alaska, a sturdy desk with a single oil lamp on it and a set of rickety kitchen equipment.

"I know the secret in growing grapes. So even when others failed, I have not and so, I don't have any worry for money. Living like a hermit, there's no one to argue with so I'm very cheerful." he said braggingly. Although he said that he was over sixty years old, I couldn't believe that he was older than my old man.

In the yard, a dark green poplar tree tosses a cool shade. "Don't you feel at ease living in place like this?" George muttered. Really, like the horse waving its tail and standing by the puddle caused by the wastewater, it sure would set my fussy mind at ease. I felt an indescribable affection for this house in the middle of a field and for its owner's life style.

Chapter 5 - Life in Camp

"Use these guys, will you, even for a week or two? You don't even have to pay them until they learn the job. Just feed them. If I ask, you're not going to refuse me are you? Ha ha!" Coming off strong, George's uncle asked the camp boss of over four hundred laborers and overseer of one and a half thousand acres, to whom he had once taught English.

"Since it's you who asks ----" the boss reluctantly agreed. We didn't feel too good about it, but at least we got work.

Should there be no work out in the country and I have to go to San Francisco, I may come down with tuberculosis living in that gloomy city. This uncertain thought I had from Alaska, now suddenly reappeared. "O sol Mio." My sun is shining over this field like boiling lead. From the ancient days of Amaterasu Ohmikami [the sun goddess], Mu of yore (see footnote 3), from the beginning of history, Sun! You are the king of the world. Breathing in your power along with the dust, what's tuberculosis!

"Are the three of you brothers?" so asked an old man next to me as he cut off spoiled grapes from the heavy bunch. Thinking to myself, "I wish you wouldn't talk to me because I'm meditating" I replied, "No, they're my friends but they are brothers". Everyone thinks we're brothers. Do we look that much alike? Of course, Sadao and Shuro-san can be brothers and Tomoko and Nellie can be sisters, so, I guess it's possible people sees us as brothers. That's right, I was praising the sun when the old man cut short my thoughts. While soaking in the sun, my feeling that had been dashed, my hope for life came boiling back up and the inflamed strength started pulsating against my rib cage.

Suffering from the excessive sun, a fantasy for her whom I had given up is revived and I start to assemble a plot for a happy novel. Shine my sun, shine! Shine brighter yet! Is there anyone who ever committed suicide during the day under the bright shining rays of the sun? Anxiety, despair and doubt all have run away to the backside of the earth, but when the sun sets in the west, they come creeping back. As the earth turns, the sun rims the field and burns red beyond the evening mist and falls into night. I put the shears away in my pocket, get on the truck and return to the camp. There, a black swarm of flies and a bed. Not a bed with a mattress but one consisting of a single futon laid over a row of boxes awaits me. Consequently, I caught a chill while sleeping, got the runs and became very thin because I had to work without being able to eat properly. I'm okay now. I bought a new futon so there's no worry of catching the chills any more.

Really, this camp is ill equipped, however, I only have to bear it for two or three more months. If I continue working, taking in the grape juice and the sun and getting darker, it's like the proverb "Koh-in, ya no gotoshi"[5]. Someone said that there's nothing as tragic as this proverb. I wonder why they say it's tragic when the days and months go by without any happy or sad feeling? Did they interpret it to mean no matter what, they saw time fly within the sight of those whose feeling were destroyed or dried up by sufferings?

---

5   Koh-in, ya no gotoshi. Direct translation is 'Light and shadow are like arrows.'
    = time flies

POSTSCRIPT

I didn't have the time to improve the phrases, nor report all that happened and it also didn't end up as a piece of art as I had highly proclaimed at the beginning. Of course, genius' like Sōseki[6] can rough draft it and come out like his masterpiece 'Kusamakura', but I have nothing to show but effort. With this, I end my report. Next, it's your turn.

How is college? How was the exhibit? Thanks for everything. Mother wrote and said two of them won. I have no comments.

Take care of yourself.

(Footnote 3) Mu was destroyed by Noah's flood. A continent in the Pacific that sank in the ocean caused by an earthquake. It's believed to have had a culture greater than that of ancient Egypt.

1932-10-15

---

6   Sōseki Natsume, - famous Japanese novelist (1885-1916) author of 'Botchan' and many other novels and books

LETTER #3

From Shirō to George Tsutakawa

My Dear George,

I received the enclosed letter so can you sent me the block prints of my 'Lake Union' and 'Gas Tanks'? If it's too bothersome, please send them a letter of declination. It's okay either way, since there's no fancy price. The reason for the rush is that the deadline was in August and when I returned from Alaska, I wrote a letter of refusal but they sent me another such letter.

If you're going to send the prints, make the address as Shiro Miyazaki, c/o George Tsutakawa with your address.

This is a good business for you. If a hundred prints are sold, you can fool me by telling me that only thirty were sold. I would then present you with the amount for fifteen of those as thanks. How about it?

I was very happy today although nothing happened to me.

When I stare into that whitish blue sky while I'm working, happiness just swells within me.

It's a happiness I alone can feel. I really believe I have benefited by coming out to the country.

Shiro

October 17, 1932

[This letter was sent from Visalia, California.]

LETTER #4

From Shirō to George Tsutakawa

George,

I received your letter that flew down here by airmail. The next day I arrived here in San Francisco. 1734 Sutter Street, San Francisco. I have taken sole possession of an air space occupied by a sunny, comfortable room and kitchen on the third floor of a house, with this number and proper name that is recognized by the post office and city hall, by paying ten dollars a month.

So now, I'll report to you what has happened, up until now. Before that though, first let me finish my business with you. Then I'll settle down and go on with my report.

"(First part omitted) -- Both of your two paintings won an award, so congratulations. The sunflower was especially well received. This year I was also lucky with both of my two entries winning. I am especially pleased that one of them, Street (Yesler Way) won first prize. As the exhibit is over, I brought back your two pictures. I'll bring them to you one of these days. - (Rest omitted).

While I was reading this letter from Nomura-san, which luckily I received only one hour before leaving the camp, I fondly thought of the goodness of this candy loving, childlike, unsophisticated man. Well anyway, before he brings the pictures to my house, in other words, as soon as possible, please go and get them from Noto Sign. Then send the 'Fish' to Atsushi and the 'Flower' to me. My room is large, bright and quiet so I want to hurry up and hang up a lot of pictures to see what the room will look like.

I received your package, which arrived safe and sound. Sorry to have troubled you when you're so busy. Thanks a lot. The two types mixed and had a strange chemical reaction. The color of the ink faded and when I wrote, it was like water. Must take more care in the future. With this, my business is finished.

Next comes my practice in composition.

George, sayonara! Eddie, sayonara! I'll notify you of my address as soon as I reach my destination. To be together only when seeking work and to leave at one's own convenience when work is gone, is a bad thing to do; however, I want to go to the city. I have to go. If I stay here, it doesn't seem that I'll be able to finish Miss Smith's Christmas card by the 10th. First off, I don't have any reference books, and on top of that, I don't have any desk or chair. I just have to get out to the city.

The Kadoya brothers said that they're going to stay in the camp till about the 10th, so we separated and I came out first. After working continuously for two months, the money I had left was forty-eight dollars and sixty-one cents. It's pitiful. In Soviet Russia, people have worked now for fifteen years without slave-like pay. How long do we have to remain in this pitiful condition? That's right, we're the only ones who can free ourselves from being slaves.

I thought of riding an American train, as I have never ridden one before. Then I thought I could save two and a half dollars, so I decided to go by stage. It doesn't matter as long as I get there. The bus quietly started to speed up with three Mexicans, carrying their meager belongs in a torn blanket and seeking a place to hibernate for the winter on board, along with another guy who worked in the same camp and was heading for San Francisco, and together with me, with trepidation of a new life (because of no money) but with aspiration,. The continuous waves of vibration made reading impossible, so I looked out of the window.

Leaving the country estate section of Visalia, the crumbling, poverty-stricken farmhouses come into view. The vineyards, forests of fig trees, orchards of oranges, peaches, pears and olives recede behind us as if being swallowed up. "Visalia valley, where we toiled every day, so long!" The bus speeds forth to a new life through the middle of the wide-open plain.

The forest of telephone poles, the rails and the highway. The three parallel lines run along the shelf of the weed filled grassland that even the cattle won't eat. If the owners would forfeit these properties, they would at least save on their taxes.

My body floats up as the bus makes a curve and drops down between red dirt banks. Under the railroad tracks, back up and curving, the pale blue sky rotates and again the three parallel lines. This is America's number one scenery.

The blue sky, the green clumps of eucalyptus trees, barns with the color of underage wine that would give you a stomachache if you drank it, the dark brown fields, the white tanks. These are American scenery Nos. 2, 3, 4, etc. Is it right to be painting these meaningless pictures that make people fall asleep? Under the red evening sky, two men go by carrying their blankets on their back. The sight of the two miserable men is like seeing an insect in late fall grasping onto a grassy leaf and waiting for death. The red sky disappeared and died before you know it. The thin moon is helplessly hooked onto the dark sky. A glaring headlight flashes by. It's dangerous! With one mistake, I don't know what would happen if it brushed against this large bus, but its not my life.

Stitching between the dark fields and country towns lighted but without any might, the bus approaches a large city. The bus stopped at the city; a capitalist's fort and the proletariat's battle field. The billboard in front of the depot says "Industrial Capital of the West, Oakland". It's a mighty town. Twenty or thirty minutes later, we reached San Francisco, a city built of stone, steel and concrete.

The first thing I noticed were posters of motion pictures, which is one of America's top three industries that we simply refers to as 'show'. 'Grand Hotel', 'Evenings For Sale', 'Secrets of the French Police', 'Call Her Savage', 'White Zombie (Adults Only)'. It's an erotic and grotesque flood. You can't help but feel the vibrations of the time. That's it! Of this panic that we are facing, it's this smelly flood, that the vast, tired and suffering petit bourgeois class is seeking while trying to hide its nervousness. What comes after this preference for the erotic and grotesque is hopelessness. An era of suicides just like it was before the Russian Revolution. Like it is now in present day Japan. Beyond this, I see a ray of hope. If suffering is pushed into an era of suicides, it's ready for an explosion. That it is not God who will save them from their suffering---

Remember I once mentioned about this guy with whom I had come here once before? That night, we slept in the apartment he knew. Next day, we went around searching for a room. I wanted to stay by myself but he begged me to let him stay with me and he would leave as soon as he finds work as a schoolboy. Since I didn't have any reason to refuse him, I accepted his request. Wherever we went, rooms with kitchen were twelve dollars a month. There was this one place with a nice room that was available for ten dollars if I was alone. I thought I could settle down here but the guy said, "let's go see the Methodist Church dormitory", so we left. It's in the white district with a splendid view from the window and is quiet. The room rent is seven and a half dollars. It even had kitchen equipment to cook with, so the guy said, "Let's decide on here". I had the feeling, however, that I wouldn't feel settled down there. Somehow it didn't feel like I would be using the room with my earned money, but felt more like I'm receiving assistance. To begin with, I didn't like the house rules that were posted on the wall. I tore one off the wall, so I'll copy it here.

SAN FRANCISCO METHODIST DORMITORY RULES

Rule #1   This dormitory is a Christian family belonging to the San Francisco Methodist Church.
Rule #2   (-omitted-)
Rule #3   The pastor is appointed supervisor of this dormitory.
Rule #4   Obey the following rules.

1. A prospective renter requires proper introduction.
2, 3, & 4   (-omitted-)
5. Residents shall attend Sunday morning services and dormitory meetings.
6. Residents shall create a dormitory atmosphere by showing respect, be honest, upright and friendly.
7. No drinking, smoking, card playing or swearing is allowed.
8. When necessary, resident may be expelled without reason.

The manager of this dormitory said that these rules don't really matter as he smoked a cigarette. Also church attendance wasn't necessary. On top of that, the guy I came with was so insistent, although I didn't like it, we had a mover bring our luggage from the stage depot. The suitcases and the kohri [wicker trunks] filled the room. A rickety single bed. To sleep on it with this guy would be like being on a trip and I can't settle down. To think that the ten dollar room had a big bed with springs.

The manager took me to the pastor whom he called "sensei".

"Do you know Reverend "X" in Seattle?"

"No, I don't."

"How about Reverend "Y"?"

"I've never been to church, so I don't know anybody." It's best to make things clear on this sort of matter.

"This is the manager, so listen to the rules and follow them."

With that, it was over. I should not have come and joined this group. I should never have come here. Not only can't I settle down, but being supervised by the manager. Or if someone should burn my mail and just say "sorry" would be terrible. So I said to myself, "Rather than wait to be expelled without reason, it's much better to excuse myself out first".

"I'm leaving here."

"If you stay here, it's only three and a half bucks per person. If you go there, it's going to cost you another six."

"I can't settle down here. I'm leaving." Finally, the guy agreed and we had to hire the mover again. It was after 7:30 P.M. in the evening when we finally settled in this room where I'm now writing this letter.

I'm getting pretty tired to where I can't think what to write anymore, so I'll end it briefly. Today is Sunday and we couldn't do any grocery shopping so we'll start cooking from tomorrow. Tonight I'm thinking of making out a rough draft of my new life in San Francisco. Come the end of next May, I'll probably be penniless except for the money I've put aside for the passage to

Alaska, but that's okay. Only this way, will I be able to throw away my petit bourgeois ideology. Then, for the first time, we are able to grasp the power to fight and free the proletariats. "Idea does not conceive reality, but reality conceives idea." I am now turning because my life has changed. I'm going to study.

It's effort! Ideology! Class struggle! You're probably oblivious to all of this. Maybe that's all right, but effort, don't forget that word.

Take care. Stay healthy and go to school. Give my regards to your father and mother, older sister Sadako, (Hi)deko-chan and to Tomi-bōh too.

Shirō

P.S. There are some splendid things in your writing. Almost amazing for one who doesn't read a lot.

I forgot to mail this letter, so I'll continue writing.

When I contemplate my new life, my heart becomes light, like something just bought at a ten cent store. The delight, like a ray of spring sunshine, fills me with emotion and while I'm walking down the brightly decorated streets with Christmas decorations, carrying a new yet cheap cooking utensil I had just bought, it seemed that this world is not so bad after all.

Whoops, it's too late. That tormenting rhythm has torn off the dreamlike happiness from me. I don't know what music it was, the radio in front of Sherman-Clay [music store] was scattering the tormenting sound. I ordered my hearing senses to sabotage it and walked briskly by, however, it was to no avail. The happiness got away from me. Money, for a guy like me, who can't have the ambition to make money, ever, unless a revolution arises.

When I awoke this morning, I remembered whiling away time without getting out of bed and that I repeatedly wrote her name on the fresh wallpaper with my ugly fingertip that was like my warped mind. The name of the girl whom I couldn't even approach because of my own shyness.

Seattle and that girl. Isn't it I who is trying to continue wandering the world from corner to corner? And yet, nevertheless, I cling forever to one without having a chance. It's true. If I keep listening to that music, I'll go crazy. Hope and strength will abruptly leave me. Yet, I don't want to break that record. Even though there is no chance, I don't want to give up. It's petit bourgeois spirit. It's pitiful.

Going without breakfast, I get by with a ten-cent meal for lunch, with herring and vegetables for supper. When you think of how cheap I can get, I order a book costing over thirty dollars at a crack. Looking back at this sort of action, even I can see a touch of craziness. It's a world where people forgo even five-cent cigarettes so they can play Hana or Shikō [Japanese gambling games] with several dollars or tens of dollars. I don't think I'm the only one with a touch of craziness. Time itself has become crazy. The sad expression of the child in the poster with Human Service written on it, or the sad, worrisome face of a woman in deep thought, standing alone by a large café entrance and handing out menus. They are the faces of the time.

Effort, effort, effort. Even though I try telling myself, there is no response. While going out to buy a paper, I'll cool off my head.

I can't write anymore. The letter this time was very bad. I think I'll go see an art exhibit tomorrow morning. Then I start working.

'Storm over Asia' will be shown here this Saturday, so I'm going to go see it. It seems to have used new technologies that after seeing it, one man said, "Art from now on will have movies at its center". Not only this, Swait's [phonetic] art is developing very fast.

[This letter was sent from 1734 Sutter Street, San Francisco. It is not dated but George Tsutakawa had noted December 1932 on it.]

LETTER #5

From Shirō to George

Evening of January 5th, 1933

From Shiro Miyazaki

To my dear George,

Letter No. X

Thanks for the 'Fish' and 'Flowers'. Also thanks for the block prints.

In order to have the 'fish' prepared, I took it to the picture frame store. The 'flowers' are making the room more cheerful. Also thanks for your letter.

Also thanks to your mother for the Christmas present and paints. I waited anxiously for that parcel No.1. The reason why was that I received it five days after parcel No.2 arrived, so it made me that much more happier. Also, as long as the plane hadn't crashed, my letter must have crossed yours and should now be in your hands.

The end. Of the first chapter.

Chapter 2

"There are two kinds of 'jinrui' (see footnote 1). 'Jinrui No.1' wastes the year's very first step, New Year's Day, by drinking and eating. In other words, celebrating. 'Jinrui No.2' spends a certain portion of that time to make plans for the year (See footnote 2). I was feeling warm and was fooling around from the next day, for fortunately I had made work plans for not one year but for the rest of my life, when a strange thing happened. That is to say, from New Year's Day until yesterday (the 4th), I only dreamt twice. There hasn't been a night I didn't dream and I didn't stay up all night. It's like a dream. Sorry to have bored you.

Boring stories continue. This is just the beginning. Is it, I'm sorry to be so boring, or is it because I'm lonely? At times, I have to rush out of the room and nihilistically, (from here, read out loud with rhythm):

Guru-guru-guru, chira-chira chira,   [Around and round and round, twinkle, twinkle, twinkle.]

Guru-guru chira-chira.   [Around and round, twinkle, twinkle.]

Guru-chira, guru-chira, guru-chira.   [Around, twinkle, around, twinkle]

Guru-chiru, guru-chiru,   [Around, scatter, around, scatter.]

Chira-chira, guru-guru.   [Twinkle, twinkle, around and around.]

Walking around in the empty darkness under the street light

Bending my ankle on the hard pavement,
Bending it again and walking around
Dragging my hurting feet and empty head on the pavement
Guru-chira, guru-chira   [Around, twinkle, around, twinkle.]
Selecting a ten cents bottle of perfume
At a ten cents store, this young man in black tuxedo,
A girl is looking for cream from a pile for clearance.
Guru-chiru, guru-chiru
Where are you going, young man with the perfume,
The seemingly poor girl who bought the cream?
Guru-chiru, guru-chiru,
Where are you going?
You, you, you. Me, me, me.
Where are we going?
Hurry and go home! Go home!
Guru-chiru, guru-chiru,
And good night.
No, no, It doesn't look like I can sleep.
Guru-chiru. .

Guru, guru, guru
Red. Yellow. White. Black. Red.
Guru-guru-guru.
Guru, guru, guru
M-O-V-I-E.
Guru-guru-guru.

Guru, guru, guru
Whorls of, whorls of light.
Guru-guru-guru.
Mo-tion pic-ture
S-H-O-W
Mo-tion pic..
Guru-guru-guru.

Whorls of, whorls of light
Whirl around, whirl around
Guru-guru-guru.
Expressionless, twenty, thin, beauty, a yellow ticket.
A tall man (wearing) a black (suit) with yellow (stripes)
A torn tic(ket).
Gohhhhh, gohhhhh,(p.pianissimo to pianissimo)   [the Japanese
    rumbling sound]
Gohhhhh, gohhhhh., (to forte) Dohhhhh, dohhhhh,   [another
    rumbling sound]

Go-gohhhhh, doh.doh.dohhhhh,(forte)

Clouds, clouds, Storm, Lightning,
No! Fall, fall,
It's an avalanche from under the balcony. Fall!
Smoke, smoke, smoke.
A lump, smoke, muku-muku   [billowing]
Doh, doh,(forte) Muku, muku.   [billowing]
Smoke, smoke, Moving, Round, Smoke,
Steel helmet, smoke, Soldier, soldier.
Flashing, thundering, dohhhhh, dohhhhh. (forte)
Flying, flash, crack, exploding,
Dohhhhh, doh-gahhhhhn. (forte to fforte)   [Sound of explosions]
Mountain, crumbles.
Dohhhhh, dohhhhh, dohhhhhhhhhhhhhhhn

The quiet mountain range of the Alps,
A peaceful mountain village, an innocent home.
Bells, the sound of bells.
An ominous sound, footsteps, foot, foot, steps, steps.
War! War! an innocent home, torn to bits.
Trenches, Shells, explosions, snow, avalanche,
Frozen to death, Night raids.
Giri, giri, giri. (pp)   An underground sound.
Gouging out the boulder, Drill, drill, drill. (pianissimo)
da--dynamite.
Giri-giri-giri,   [scrapping sound]
giri-giri-giri, giri-giri-giri.
giri-giri-giri, giri-giri-giri.   (forte)
Giri-giri-giri, giri-giri-giri,
giri-giri-giri. giri-giri-giri,   (ff)
The noise, stops. Stillness, uneasiness, dynamite, death.

A command, defend the country, silence, uneasiness,
Uneasiness, uneasiness, death, death.
D-O-O-M-E-D B-A-T-T-A-L-I-O-N
Curtain (see footnote 4)

WAR, INSANITY, CRAZY, CRAZY......
POISON GAS, EXPLOSION, EXPLOSION, GAS, GAS, GAS.

Death, death, tragic death, I do not want to die.
War, terror, Everyone is crazy.
Wake up! Wake up! Why do you fight?
Useless war, useless, cruel, useless.
Why do you fight? Wake up!

Look! Those soldiers, those sailors who fought the pirates.

Those cowboys, those gangsters,
None are afraid of death like you, to be killed.
Coward! I'm a coward. a coward, a coward.
I am a coward. I am a coward.

- - -"Don't emphasis so much of your cowardice" (see footnote 5)
This coward, this crazed man, inhaling in the night air,
will now go indoors and go to sleep. (see footnote 6)

23

Footnotes:

1. To be in tune with your letter that had the phrase 'a Jinshu called Japanese'. [Jinshu is normally translated as 'race' as in a race of people. Shirō, in his letter says 'Jinrui' which is normally translated as mankind, a race (of people), or a type (or group) of people.]
2. This phrase on the page one of the January 1st issue of the newspaper.
3. From here, I sort of copied the technique from a chapter of Joyce's "Ulysses".
4. If I don't write as audaciously as this, I can't release my pent up feeling of this town.
   While I was writing this, my head rattled and ached just like when I walk the downtown streets. I must make my body stronger.
5. A phrase from a novel I was about to return to the library.
6. "There's another man within me that angry with me" Sir Thomas Browne.

It's only nine o'clock. I'll write a little more.

Chapter 3

"If I was in that Sing Sing prison, I would have had turkey for Christmas."
"Really. Rather than being honest and starve, it's much wiser to eat turkey in a prison."
"Really. Nappa and sardines, nappa and sardines, nappa and sardines. It's not thankful."
"Sardine, sardine, sardine. It's sardine every day and you know, something like a pimple, one....two...."
"Don't get so angry. I just want to know how to cook."

"Next time you send a letter to George, write 'Every time you send me a letter, can you include a recipe or two of some simple cooking?'"
"Say, that's good."
"Hey, shall I make some "zenzai'? [Sweet red bean paste soup]
"You've gotta be kidding! That leaves no pot. Can't cook any rice. I can't take it if I have to eat 'zenzai' for two whole days. If it hadn't been for the

people in the next room or those downstairs giving us 'sushi', I probably would have suffocated with the 'zenzai'."

"I'll make something with the sardines."

"But sardine is the cheapest."

"Why don't we cook some beans?"

"Yeah, that's okay."

"Hey, will you feed me some 'miso' soup?

That's okay too. I'll start making the soup stock.

Oh sardines, sardines, good bye sardines."

A pleasant dinner conversation. (Man within me). When I get lonesome, I start talking to the other me, the other two mc's. It's good company when I go out to paint and have to walk for some distance.

Speaking about painting, I had a terrible mishap the other day. I went into a ship-building yard and sketched a huge massive shiny gray crane and thought to myself that it was pretty good. When I went to the exit, a guard who wasn't there when I went in, confiscated my picture. He told me, "absolutely no pictures or photographs". When I asked him to give me back my picture, he snorted, "If you don't leave in two minutes, I'll have you thrown in!" I tried asking to two more minutes, but it didn't do any good, so I returned home whistling to myself. Darn!

I thought I'd talk to you about motion pictures. It's only 10 o'clock. I'll continue.

Chapter 4

No. 1 Storm Over Asia
No. 2 Doctor X
No. 3 Madchen (Maiden) in Uniform
No. 4 As You Desire Me
No. 5 Doomed Battalion

These are the ones I remember among those I saw since coming here from Visalia.

Movie No.1 is a Soviet movie of three or four years ago. They showed this at a hall on an approximately 4-1/2 feet square screen, so it didn't have the impact of that shown in a regular theater; however, when the Mongolian and Red Army started to win over the British Forces, the kids and adults, both clapped their hands. It was like watching a motion picture in a schoolyard in Japan. Although it was a silent picture, the accompanying amplified, recorded music gave it strength.

The No.2 film was in natural color. The terror scenes all had a blue hue while the happy scenes used bright colors, a method of illustration unattainable with black and white. Just like talkies pushed aside silent films, it will become a colored film world, but it's still not that good.

No.3 is a German movie that has been shown in the world's major cities for more than twenty or thirty straight weeks. They all seemed to admire it. I couldn't understand it and want to see it again.

No.4. First time I saw Greta Garbo. In this movie, her metallic-like beauty was good, but I thought the composition of every scene was also good.

No.5. I thought it was good in every point. It moved me the most.

I believe movies to be at the pinnacle of the arts. I believe they will be able to incorporate all of the progress made by science, music, painting, poetry and literature. Try to remember and compare

Shōnosuke Onoe works, the one you saw when you were a kid in Japan and the present. How much advancement will there be in the next ten years? When I went to see No.3, they also showed a movie of about twenty years ago. When I compare that with No.3, it's like the difference between a monkey's brain and a human's. Ten years from now, how much do you think, color, sound, picture taking equipment and skill will have advanced? Artists will have to look forward for the advancement of filmmaking and cooperate with it.

Chapter 5

"My daughter, even though she's only twelve, is taller than her mother. Spending the summer in the north and winter in Florida, there is no stopping growth because of bad climate, I'm making a race of six and a half foot people." writes a bragger. "For us, to transfer is unthinkable. My younger sister wrote, "I have a little cold". When winter comes, she's always catching cold. If you go to Florida, you can't catch cold even if you tried". I hope Hideko-chan gets well soon. You take care of yourself, too. Go to bed as soon as you get out of the bath, like before.... Since I'm alone, I'm taking care not to get sick.

Well, give my regards to all.

Looking like this, I (happily) read you letter and opened your gift. [A small snapshot was attached to the letter]

Sayonara.   Good-bye.

Trying not to lose to you, I'm also writing on the backside of this letter.

P.S. Thanks for your critique of my Christmas Card. Should I have made the street white and the letters black? I did it that way on the first block, but the result wasn't very good.

Even though I had bought it, I didn't know how the frame for the 'Sunflower' was. I had thought it was a bit darker. To me, it shines too much. You said that painting has strength but that's not so. If I had a little more time and spent at least two days, it probably would have come out better. Still, the room has become livelier. This summer when I go back, I'll bring you a better one as a present.

Your 'fish' will be cooked the day after tomorrow.

Thank you, in your busy schedule, once more.

If you're busy, you don't have to write, (although I won't be thankful if you shut me out or leave me alone). Even so, when my school starts, I won't be able to write long ones like this. School starts January 9th. Good-bye.

It must have been rough reading.
Regards to everyone once again.

It's 11:22 P.M., however, I can't rely on my watch. Yet more follows:

I sent your Christmas Card to Kadoya the day before the previous letter, since I found their Los Angeles address. They sent you theirs before they received yours.

Next month, the museum is exhibiting nothing but prints. I haven't gone yet. This town has a lot more sculptures than Seattle. Ones that are no less than 'The Aging Man'[?], are in downtown and in the parks.

"To be happy', 'Not to be happy'. Your Christmas present 'Atelier' [a Japanese art magazine] may not get there for some time. I ordered it in November but the bookstore often makes mistakes or the post office loses them. Just recently a three volume 'Cezanne' picture collection disappeared. So, don't look forward for it, nor lose hope. It's best to just forget about it.

[This letter was sent from 1734 Sutter Street, San Francisco]

LETTER #6

From Shirō to George

Until yesterday, the last two, three days were cold.

Looking out from the school hallway, the fast running rain clouds were racing down from north to south, so didn't Seattle also have bad weather?

Today, I finished the second week of school. If I write out a week's program, it's like this:

Cast drawing (morning)	11 hours (4 x 1/2 day)
Still life drawing (afternoon)	11 hours
Landscape drawing	3 hours (half day)
Human body sketch	Half day
Anatomy	1 hour
History of Art	1 hour

The teacher for History is on a trip so we haven't had any lessons, but will probably start next week. I'm having a hard time with still life drawing. Cast drawing is fun and will be useful. When I was drawing each little shadow, the teacher opens up and starts telling me, "get a bigger grasp of the subject and draw. Express it with beauty. To start to draw with black and white is fun and enjoyable. Isn't that right?" "Why can't you draw any better? " It seemed as if he thought that if I studied hard for two years, I would be able to draw like Michelangelo, but I just shrugged my shoulders and didn't say anything. Not only this teacher, but all of the teachers at this school explain things artistically.

The other day when I was listening to a lecture entitled, "Color and hues for artists", what he said (not about the content but the way he explained it) and his body movements, was like watching a play. The content, however, was about the science of color, just the opposite of what you would call artistic. It was an explanation of the scientific principle of color and he made clear how artists such as Cezanne, Goya, Van Gogh, cubists and surrealists incorporated the principle in their works. The conclusion is that our duty is to study and absorb the discoveries of the past and add on new things and pass it on to the next generation. (According to Tadashi Itō, newness in artwork is one that has a higher degree of expressive effect.)

Listening to this lecture, I believe that, eventually, color-hues will all be numbered. Instead of "give me a yellow" or a red, there will be a day when we'll buy art paint by saying, "Give a tube of No.30", or "Give me a tube of No. 125". It'll be so much more convenient that way; however, paint manufacturing must progress a lot more before this will happen.

This school is quite different from my Garfield High School. To begin with, there is no bell. You start when you like and quit when you like. It is very free. There are times when the teacher is absent. And then, the facilities are complete, especially the library, although you can't take the books home. When I first went there, they brought out and showed me the art collection of Fujita. When I was reading Takeshi Kimura's book, it stated, "In essence, Fujita transferred the skill of Japanese art to oil and was thought of as a curiosity in art circles over there (France)", but when I saw his drawings at an exhibit recently, I couldn't believe that. When compared with other great artists, he has the ability that is not inferior.

Speaking of exhibits, there was one showing forty to fifty Soviet prints. Maybe it's because I saw it with jaundiced eyes, but they looked good. They are all assiduous works and it appeared to show their constructive spirit in their technique. I saw another work (not a painting but a movie) called "Kameradschaft", based on similar socialistic ideology. It was a complete work from all points of view with no deficiencies. I never saw such a good picture. The person in front of me said, "Very interesting!", while a lady beside me said to herself, "That's a good propaganda!" This movie taught me to "draw and separate light and haze. Life is also an art!" (Ibsen's words).

In yesterday's still life class, the day after the lecture on color and hue, the students were having a heated debate. The problem was, when you place a complimentary color A on B, whether or not you should try out each time what percent blue, what percent yellow, what percent white on the color wheel. It ended up that since there is no color wheel, nothing could be done. Maybe in ten years, they will have a color wheel in each classroom.

When I awoke this morning, it was 9 o'clock so I skipped the landscape class and read about dialectical materialism. I thought dialectic was body rhythm that I had heard in anatomy. In other words, a dialectic, where history and society all move like contradiction, unification, contradiction, unification and a body with a cyclic rhythm such as

contradiction	contradiction
unification	unification

The afternoon class was anatomy sketch, so I sketched a boxer. Last week was a fisherman. In this class, many women in their forties and fifties come and as if they are proud of being near sighted, draw with their eyes close to their paper.

The above is a simple report on the school.

Regards to all.

January 20, 1933   Shirō

To George

[Mailing address was 1734 Sutter Street, San Francisco. In a formal Japanese letter. The date, the sender and the recipient's name are always at the end of the letter as seen above.]

[Translation of a note written on the program for the movie "Kamerradschaft (Comradeship)" is attached to the letter.]

The explanation (subtitle) was in English, but it would have been much more interesting if I could have understood the conversation that was in French and German.

[The following is a note on the next attraction "Der Raub Der Mona Lisa (The Theft of Mona Lisa)" in the same program.]

I think this movie handles the passion of the youth that steals the Mona Lisa with a Freudian psychoanalysis. I want to go see it but you know (how it is).

LETTER #7

From Shirō to George

Dear Geo,

Today I received a critique of my block print. His name is W.S.G. who lives at 1902-8W, Seattle, but I don't know who he is. If you know what kind of a guy he is, won't you let me know. Please. ASAP. NOW!

Speaking about block prints, can I leave my scrapbook of block prints at your place? Until the revolution is over?

According to the blue newspaper, it's "Good times come next spring". This will be my sixth year-end down here.

Well then, I ask you to hurry on the above requests. Even though you're so busy.

December 28th, 1934

[This letter was mailed from 1538 Post Street, San Francisco.

W.S.G. refers to Dr. William S. Gamble.]

LETTER #8

From Shirō to George

Happy New Year!

My picture won an award but I hardly feel the New Year spirit.

Thank you. You sent me all of the things I wanted.

Give my regards to your mother. Friendship is really a warm thing.

My regards also to WSG and give him my thanks. I want to send him a reply one of these days but tell him I recommend that he first join the Artists and Writers Union.

Are you still going to school? When you finish reading the novel of my helpful friend, "Why did he enter Elewa?", please write your impressions. This was my maiden novel.

The 'Ex Libris' you sent was good, but the other two works are starting to lose the poetry that you once had. Man should not lose his poetry. Especially an artist without poetry, in painting, music, novel or poem, is not worth looking at. In poetry, only the proletarian type has growth and strength. Bourgeois type poetry is sick and abnormal.

I'd like to return to Seattle very much but don't have the opportunity. Springtime in Seattle is really pretty. I want to go back, but there is nothing I can do.

The Pacific shore of San Francisco has a sandy beach stretching fifteen miles or so. Last Sunday, I was walking there with a friend and talking. After the revolution, let's go up to the Northwest. Let's make a boat during our vacation and go up to Alaska. Then you'll be one of the crew too.

I saw Nomura's picture at the Legion last year. His recent works have completely worsened. To live in a bourgeois' poem, 'is akin to 'dodo no tsumari' [frequent clogging].

Have you ever seen a Soviet movie? If they ever come to Seattle, no matter what, be sure to take your family and go see it. That music! That lighting, composition, strong movement and rhythm. When you see a Soviet film, you will know why only the proletariats develop in politics, economics and arts.

If capitalism progresses, it'll become like Germany with starvation and terrorism. For us who work to eat, the way is with the free and constructive Soviets.

To be in capitalism's last panic with it's nearing destruction, it's hard to fall in love. Even though many have reached twenty-five or thirty years of age, they are still alone. Be as they may, at least I do not want to lose your friendship. It probably won't be long before everyone awakens and open their eyes.

I plan to change my lodging within a couple of days. I'll send you the new address then.

Thanks for all of the various things you sent me.

How is your mother's health?

To Geo.   Shirō

[No date or address given]

[Note: I had trouble translating the phrase "dodo no tsumari" mainly because he wrote 'dodo' in katakana (Japanese alphabet and not in kanji (Chinese characters). It's difficult to visualize what he actually meant because it does not seem to connect to the first half of the sentence 'If you live in a bourgeois' poem'. Tsumari is a blockage or stoppage. Dodo means 'to dwell excessively on' or 'to say repeatedly'. Another 'dodo' with different Chinese characters means often or frequently. Also there is the dodo bird, but I don't think he meant that, or did he? Maybe, 'there is no progress' is the right translation.]

LETTER #9

From Shirō to George

George, I thank you. I found out after I asked you but I didn't have to pay the whole semester's fee at one time, so I went to school yesterday evening and paid just one month's tuition. Therefore, I'll be able to get along somehow, so even though you busted your back in your busy schedule to send me the money, I sent the money back to you. Please don't think ill of me.

After five years, I tried drawing at school, but couldn't draw at all. It's starting all over from the beginning again. I went to the public library today and borrowed Michelangelo and copied one. Eventually, after I accumulate them for a month or two, I'll send you all my drawings, so please look at them.

Recently, I have seen plenty of landscapes I'd like to paint, but I decided to concentrate on drawing for the time being.

On the way home from the library, I thought to myself, Michelangelo draws each muscle and the picture is very romantic, but in contrast, Van Gogh draws in his style and is very realistic.

Take some photos of your pictures and send them to me. I want to see them. I'm impressed you quit drinking. Isn't it bad for the body to quit all at once?

I drew one watercolor. I'll send it to Bill this week. Somehow the picture is missing coherence. Saying that, all of my pictures are missing coherence. If I strengthen one or two main characters and weaken the rest, I can get unity; however, it appears to me that everything that goes into the picture have their own individuality. Even if I keep on drawing that way, eventually I think I will find a way to get unity.

George, don't go back to Japan and leave me. And by all means come on down. It's been a while and I'd like to leisurely talk to you and Bill.

The rain has stopped and it has become like autumn. With that, the worry of unemployment has also come.

Shirō

[No date or address]

Letter #10

From Shirō to George

George!

Sorry I haven't written for a long time. The start of my letter is always the same. Then, when I do write, it's because I have something for you to do. This time, it's sort of a different business. You must be busy but please take a pen to hand and let me know within a week on the following matters.

I'm just starting to write a great ambitious novel that will take about two months. What I want to know is:

Concerning the cannery union. It appears, all of those from Seattle were union members.
a. How did they join?
b. What was the connection between the cannery contractors and the union?
c. The method used in the union activities. A brief history.
d. What benefits were had by joining the union, etc. and whatever else you know.
   When Furuya Bank went bankrupt, a delivery boy who worked for Furuya Grocery committed suicide but how did he do it? Also about any other tragedies that occurred when the bank went bankrupt.
   When the anti-Japanese activities started, what sort of boycott or exclusion did the farmers experience? Give one or two examples.
4. The street name where the Atlas Theater is located.

It's a lot but please do it for me.

My current status? For nigh onto three months, I've been working in a salad making company, twelve hours a day making twenty-one dollars a week. It's no fun but it can't be helped. When I say salad, I don't know if they have any in Seattle, but it's cut-up vegetables placed in a cellophane bag and distributed to grocery stores. It appears business is very good and when compared to the time I started, it has grown three or four times.

Don't worry about my going to Alaska that I asked you about. It looks like I'll be able to go from San Francisco although it seems pretty difficult because I'm getting it through the union. Anyway, if I don't go to Alaska, I won't be able to buy a car. The city of Los Angeles is so wide that you can't do anything without one. If I get a car I'll make a leisurely trip back to Seattle. Just to see what the girl I like is doing! I think she should be living somewhere near your grocery. I'm telling you in advance, I'm not going back to see a lazy guy like you.

Kidding aside, I had the Consumer Union Report sent directly to you. Read it. You'll learn to spend your money wisely. In this type of capitalistic world where it's okay to sell a can full of rocks, I really felt the necessity of reading this type of honest do-gooder organization report. Your membership will expire in June so you shouldn't have to worry about it until then.

Until next time. Please answer my request.

Are you healthy? You sure there isn't a big growth by your neck again? If you leave such a thing around, all of you customers will run away!

Regards to all. Excuse the scribbling and abusive words.

Shirō

April 1st

[No address or year is given. George had marked it 4-1-40, however, from other letters, the year must be in error as it would put him at the camp near Sacramento where he had written two letters of 3-27-40 and 4-4-40. Comparing the context of other letters, it appears to be 1937 or earlier.]

LETTER #11

A postcard from Shirō to Bill Gamble

Shirō Miyazaki
305 E. 2nd St.
Los Angeles, Cal.

Mr. W.S. Gamble
1902 8th W
Seattle, Wash.

Dear Bill:

I safely arrived in L.A. two days ago.

I really thank you for your hospitality during my stay in Seattle.

I should write a long one but am somewhat busy.

Please give my kind regard to your brother and Miss Margaret.

Yours very sincerely
S.M.

[The postcard is stamped June 10, 1937, right after his return from Seattle where he attended our mother's funeral. According to Dr. Gamble, this was the first time they met.]

[The post card had a photo of a desert scene with Joshua trees in the foreground and Mt. San Jacinto (near Palm Springs) in the background.]

Letter #12

A post card from Shirō to George

[A part of the text is obliterated (denoted by (xxxx)) by the postal cancellation stamp.]

Hello George

Tonight I went and saw the Konoye and Michio Itō combi[nation][7]. [xxxx] was "New World", [xxxx] and "Blue Danube", I thought it was [xxxx] but didn't care too much for it. Yet it was very popular and the Bowl was full of people and [xxxx]. World famous conductors come here and they let you hear them for a cheap admission price of fifty or seventy-five cents, so I'm very thankful.

Various things happened. First, my car broke down so I replaced it. Had an accident and the other guy was injured pretty bad. As he was drunk, it was fortunate for me.

Our union changed from AFL to CIO. It's because AFL got twenty-five thousand dollars from Safeway Co. and sold us [down the river]. I'm working every day as a cashier at a produce store. I work ten hours a day and the commuting time is an hour and a half, round trip. I hate it. Every night, it's lack of sleep. I got a publisher for my novel but I don't have much time to write. I feel like I'll be able to write a pretty good one.

The Soviet film "Last Night" was very good.

The picture on this post card is a souvenir of the Hollywood Bowl and they say they once had over thirty thousand in attendance. You can hear very well, even if you're in the last row. I'll write again.

---

7   Konoye is believed to be the conductor of the Nippon Symphony Orchestra and Michio Itō was a noted koto player.

My regards to ojisan [George's father], obasan [George's mother] and Bill.

Shirō

It's wonderful to listen to the symphony at the Bowl, laying on the bench and looking up at the moon and the stars.

It's been a week now since I wrote this and left it on the desk. Please forgive my heartlessness.

The postmark on the card is dated August 28, 1937 with a return address of Schiro Miyazaki 305 E. 2nd Street, Los Angeles, California which is in the center of Little Tokyo district.]

LETTER #13

From Shirō to Bill Gamble

Jan. 11th, 1938
1616 E. 1st St.

My Dear Bill:

I thank you for your letter and all the troble for my painting to send it to the exhibition. I admire the way you work and study. More power to you!

The year, 1937, has gone busily, and busily came 1938. Last year we did shortened two hours in our food market field, until then we were working 12 hours now we work ten hours, and this year we will make it eight hours a day through out union. With these ditail report, I sent to George on the Christmas a first part of our novel which my friend and I wrote, my poems in Japanese, my small block prints and a wood cuts of a Spanish Worker fighting against facism and a drawing of a Soviet Worker, both of which were made by Rockwell Kent for the New Masses and the Sunday Worker. I did not get any letter from George. So I have been wondering whether he is very ill or not. Since there is no mention in your letter about it, I think he is very busy or very very lazy.

I think that it is imposible for me to paint or make cuts, for I make myself busy in the union work (of couse after ten hours work in a market) and writing stories. By the way, do you go to see the movies? If not, you better see at least "The stage door (R.K.O.)" "Stand In (MGM)" "They wouldn't forget" "The Life of Emile Zola (Warner Bros.)" "100 men and a girl (United Artist)". It seems to me the movies is a symphone of the arts. We, artists and writers will be benefited by seeing motion pictures. I know you are very busy but good movies will give you as much as the visits to the exhibitions to your work. I have seen "the stage door" twice and "100 men and a girl" four times. The composition rather construction of the story of the "100 men and a girl" is perfect!

I read in paper that some times ago, a storm visited the northwest was it hard. Some times, I think of Seattle and I could continue the paintings with you and George. The beautiful silver snow covers Seattle hills. Once George and I with his uncle went in to the mountain on Jan. 2nd and we made painting and I remember that I over painted it. It was a long time ago. Once there was such a day that we planed to go to Alaska on a fishing boat for painting. Well, there'll be no end if I write this way.

On my coming day off, I am planing to attend a concert to hear Jasha Heifitz. Please tell this to George.

It is the time to go to bed, so I better finish up with more important business, that is the block I borrowed and sent to Japan. It did not come yet though we sent letters asking to send it back. I'll write once more, and hope that it'll be in time you make books.

You know it takes a long time for me to write in English. So pardon me this short letter and bad English.

I enclosed a poem written by my friend. Your oppinion on this poem is very well come.

Take care yourself.

Please give my regards to Miss. Margaret.

Yours very truly
Schiro Miyazaki

[Letter is from Los Angeles]

LETTER #14

From Shirō to Bill Gamble

Jan. 28th, 1938
1616 E. 1st St.
Los Angeles, Calif.

Dear Bill:

These prints are for the collection of yours and George's, and if you could spare a time for me please send it to the print maker's exhibition. I made it for the illustration in the Harvest. The title is "O for the fruit of labor". Give me your criticisms on that print.

Fortunately I could spent lots of time cutting this print for I got stay in my room for three weeks after an accident in which I got a crack inside of my knee cap. It is nothing to worry about. Within one or two weeks it'll be all right.

I had a letter about one week ago that your block is on the way from Japan. I will send it back as soon as I receive it. Thank you very much for the block.

Please give my regard to George.

Yours truly
Schiro Miyazaki

LETTER #15

A postcard from Shiro to George

[Portions of the text was difficult to read as the card was bend, torn and frayed.]

Hello Geo.

How is your life lately? I've been cooped up in one room for over a month and feel thoroughly disgusted. I sprained my leg but it should be better in a week or two so there is no worry. During this time, I've made a cut from an old sketch, spent some time on my novel, but most of the time, I'm sleeping or smoking.

I take it that spring has come to Seattle too. The other day, when I was taken for a drive out to the country, the larks were not singing and it felt like a strange spring.

In Seattle, if Dore loses the election and Meyers is elected[8], probably the unnecessary troubles with laborers with lessen over there too.

An acquaintance sent me this postcard. This mission has been vacant since the earthquake of 1812.

Send me a letter or postcard too.

[The postcard with a picture of Mission San Juan Capistrano was postmarked March 3, 1938. The return address was Shiro Miyazaki 1616 E. First Street, Los Angeles, California.]

---

8   According to Seattle records, John Dore was elected for the second time in 1936, but became gravely ill in April 1938 and died 5 days after the city council removed him from office. Arthur Langlie was elected mayor over Victor Meyers in a special election on April 27th, 1938.

LETTER #16

A postcard from Shirō to Bill Gamble

> Schiro Miyazaki
> c/o Mr. Kodama
> Borego Valley
>
>   San Diego County, Calif.

> Mr. William Gamble
> 1902 - 8th West
> Seattle, Wash.

> Dear Bill and George

> I am in Borego desert now with a Japanese farmer who are as good as Geo. family.

> I came thinking the hot weather is for my knee.

> The wild flowers which are is blosomes now are beautiful, but best thing in here is the desert itself.

> I want to make some cuts but I am not yet acquiented enough. It takes times you kow . I don't know how long I will stay here. May be about a month.

> Thanks for everything you have done for me in the print makers exhibition. Funiest part of it is that I don't know where about of eagle harbor.

[The post card is post marked Borego, Calif. with a date of Apr. 30, 1938. The picture side of the post card had a desert scene and a poem titled 'Mornin' On the Desert (Found written on the door of an old cabin on the desert)'.]

Letter #17

From Shirō to Bill Gamble

May 28th '38
1616 - E. 1st St.

Dear Bill

This morning I came back to L.A. I wished I could stay on the desert a little longer, but the union situation in L.A. compeled me to come back.

"The Old Greek Church" which you sent me was very good. The way you bring out the local color, the composition and cutting are wonderful. The only thing I like to say on your study of the block print is that, you better make larger cuts in size of block, so that you could put in more air, and you will meet more difficulty which will bring you more progress of technique of cutting. Try to use more variety of cuttings.

What you said for my cuts made me feel good. But if you tell me more shortcoming of my cuts I would make better one next time.

I never made a wood cut, and I am very anxious to make wood cuts. If there are any way to get the wood blocks cheaply, please let me know. If George said that I am changing the style of cutting, that is a queer thing. He should know that I never use the same technique except the four cuts which I made as a set. I was so impressed by Lynd Ward's "Wild Pilgrimage" that I am now tring after him. But I never thought that one technique of cutting will suit to all objects.

After I wrote this far, I had a trip of three days to San Francisco. We took the coast road along the Pacific which is just opened two weeks ago. The sights were wonderful. This trip gave me a longing to have a good car and to drive up to Seattle in the future.

This is a small world! That is what I thought after reading your letter which tells me that you too were in Palm Canyon. There are two Palm Canyons, one in Palm Spring and the other in Borego where I stayed.

I have no oil nor water colors and I did not took any linoleum, so I did not make any on the desert, except some sketches. I hope I will make some cuts out of them, though the desert landscape is the hardest object in black and white. I saw one oil painting in Borego post office, which looks just like a country side, not a desert. If you want to draw a desert landscape, you got stay there a long time.

I thank you for your labor and effort to arrange my one man show, but if you did

not start yet, you better not do it for you have not much time and George too. I wish you

and George will spend more time for the study of the art instead of spending precious time on my show.

Your "Mt. St.Helens" arrived the other day. I will send it as soon as I get. Thank you again for let us use that block.

Town gives me a kind of dizzy feeling. May be it is caused by the noise of the city, or the trips, or may be altogether, any way I'll stop here and day "Good-bye" to you. Please give my regard to George

Yours truly.
Shirō Miyazaki

LETTER #18

A postal card from Shirō to Bill Gamble

June 6th, '38

Dear Bill:

Just a line to inform you that I have moved to 577 S. Central Ave.
Los Angeles, Cal.

Yours
Shirō Miyazaki

Letter #19

From Shirō to George

Dear George

I don't know why but I wanted to talk with you tonight, so I'm writing this letter. I just got home from work. It's 10 P.M. Recently I've been working four days a week. I was working six days but ever since winter came, the produce section has been slow, so it became four days. So my pocket is getting lonelier, but now, I have more time and I think that may be better yet.

As a result, with these last three days off, I've been working hard on my lino blocks. I'll probably be sending you a few soon. Right now, I'm laboriously doing the engraving and it takes time. I was cutting the Desert Mountain yesterday but because I didn't do a good job in the draft drawing, it didn't go good. I discontinued and am now redrawing it. Boy, mountains are hard!

Thanks for the paints. I want to hurry up and paint but since there weren't any red, yellow or green, I'm waiting until I have some money. I should get enough if I write a novel or make a cut for the newspaper's New Year's edition. Recently, I've been doing things that it seems better if I put my effort toward art after all. I tried union activities for some years now, but I don't have the talent to merge in among the masses. Rather, it seems I can show myself better through art. So I'm going back to art again but I'm not thinking of going back to school. Of course, I want to try some more drawing but I think I can do it mostly through self-teaching. When I mention art, I think of Seattle and if I return there, I feel I will be able to absorb it better; however, there's the matter with my old man, so it's a little difficult for me to go back. It may be better that I go to New York. For the present, I'm thinking of sticking strictly with block prints. What do you think?

It must be cold up there by now. Two or three weeks ago, it got so cold that I couldn't stand it any more, so I went out and got myself an overcoat on the payment plan, but then it got warm again. It's funny.

Bill wrote in his letter that you took a vacation and went up toward the mountains. The mountains of the Northwest are great, aren't they? Did you do any sketching? Make yourself some time and do some lino cuts. Also, if you have some time, write me what's going on up there. Also around next spring, why don't you come to Southern California while taking in the Exposition in San Francisco [the 1939 San Francisco World's Fair]. I'd like to see you. To me, you are my real good friend. Even though it's been five or six years since coming down here, I haven't been able to make any friends like you.

It's almost the end of the year but this year was a bad one for me. I injured my leg right after the new year, was out of work for over half a year and during that time I wasn't doing anything but leading an idle life. Next year though, starting from now with my art, I will try for a year where I'll leave my footprints.

It's awful quiet tonight. I was talking with a customer at the store and telling him, "It's so quiet here".

In France, five million people are about to have a general strike. I hope the union wins. If the present government wins, Hitler will leap out and change the map of Europe. It'll be something terrific if five million people do strike. During the general strike in San Francisco, even though it was midday, man, it was as quiet as the middle of the night. Really, it's then when you feel the power of the working people. I think I would even like to reveal this power in my block prints. For example, when drawing a mountain or making a print of the fields.

Tomorrow is work too so I'll go to bed.

I'll be waiting for you letter. Give my regards to everybody.

Shirō

October 29th

[No address or year is given but the year is believed to be 1938 since the World's Fair at Treasure Island was in 1939.]

Letter #20

From Shirō to George

George

The other day, actually five days ago, I bumped into Eddie on the street. The next day, Eddie and George both came over and we renewed our old acquaintanceship. It's been five years. We talked an awful lot. The three of us lamented over your indolence. Send me a letter, even if it's a postcard. Write to them too.

The two of them, with another guy are partners and running a produce market. They said that business is so-so, neither good nor bad. When I told them, "it's been so long, I worried that I might mistake one for the other", they both laughed.

This is a bad year for me. I broke my leg in January, was idle until May and had to borrow money. From May, partly to recuperate, I went to stay with a farmer who lived in the desert near the Imperial Valley. The desert seems like all sand but it's nature all exposed and I loved it. But it didn't result in any money. Around June, the union weighed on my mind so I came back, even though I wanted to stay longer. The town was depressed worse than ever. I finally found work and that at a place forty miles away, round trip. I went to work there waking up at six, but in the third week, I lost my job and became unemployed again. The boss had sold his market and the new owner fired all of the Japanese and replaced them with Whites. Somehow, this is an unlucky year. Although I don't have any work, I'm staying at a friend's hotel. By helping around, I don't have to worry about eating or sleeping. When your pocket is empty though, the whole body also feels empty and you don't have any pep.

When September comes, the schoolboys, who are upsetting the job market, will be going back to school, so there should be work then. The schoolboys work for only ten to fifteen dollars. We don't work for less than twenty. The bosses hire what's cheaper. Such being the case, I haven't been to Hollywood Bowl even once this year.

Where I'm now staying, there's a train stop as well as a streetcar barn nearby, so when I have enough to buy some canvas, I think I'll paint one or two canvases. When I was talking to the Kadoya brothers about Seattle, I got the urge to paint. That's how much Seattle is alive within me. If only things had gone well between my old man and me, I would be living in Seattle.

Produce markets have no business during winter. Eventually, as a result of Roosevelt's Recovery Act, things should get a little better.

I haven't written to Gamble for a long time, but how is he doing? Please give him the English poem I have enclosed.

LETTER #21

From Shirō to Bill Gamble

577 S. Central Ave.
L.A. Calif.
Sept. 14th, 1938

Dear Bill:

Thank you for your letter. It was swellest letter I have ever had a chance to read. It was a powerful poem. Please do not mistake, although people used to refer poems as a kind of dreams, whenever I say poem it means the rythmical feeling of a person based on the reality not on the dream.

You have been working very hard, Don't you? Please keep it up, and in same time take care of yourself too.

For me too, past two weeks were busy days. We were on picket line fighting unfair labor practice of a chane of 30 stores in Los Angeles. As the result of this we will be able to increase about 10,000 dollars per month in their wages among Japanese workers in this city. You know that workers must be organized. It will give more human feelings to the people of the lower depth, and it will keep the circulation of the money and keep out the economical crisis longer.

Yes, there is no worries in our friendship, for we, you and I, both have the spirit of love and sacrifice. Whether you believe in God and I believe in the conscience does any difference to me. We were, we are, and we will be a very close friend.

You wrote a great deal good things about me, but I am afread it is a over estimation of my ability. I know myself that I have not enough criative ability in the field of fine art. I am thinking may be I can do a better job in the field of writing stories on novels. Only the troble is that I have not enough experiences to write. Zola did published a novel at my age, that is at 28, but for me I need at least one half decade more to start writing. Meanwhile I'll stick to the union movement. Although I am not type to fit to it. We are now working with the company union. It is one of the most difficult job in the union movement.

By the way, have you ever study the history of arts in connection with the economical and political history. If you do, you will find out that Beethoven was great because not only he had ability to express his feeling on his musical sheets, but he possessed the ability to grasp the spirits of raising capitalism in nineteenth century. So Zola was. If you understand this relationship between the basic stracture of society that is economy and the uper stractures that is arts, moral, politics and so forth, I am sure that it'll bring great change to your paintings and prints, and it'll give more power to your works

Cezanne is great not because he created something new, but he put the spirits of the republican, democrasy and raising tide of capitalism which most of artists at that time could not grasp, in his still-life, landscapes and others.

After I wrote this much, I began to read "From Bryan to Stalin" by Bill Foster, he wrote in the preface:

"In the earlier stages of its development, the world capitalist system played a historically progressive role. Based upon a more advanced method of production that feudalism which preceded it, capitalism raised cultural levels and attained a higher stage of society. It is true that these advances were made at the cost of tremendous exploitation of the working masses in all countries; yet this era of capitalism constituted a definite step forward to a richer and fuller life.

But capitalism has now exhausted its progressive role; it is no longer a stimulus to social advance but a brake upon it. Caught in a hopeless contradiction between an expanding productive apparatus and shrinking markets this social system has fallen into an acute state of degeneracy and reaction."

I praised Zola and Beethoven, because they fought with their arts for this capitalism against the feudalism. Wagner will be better example; he fought not only with his opera such as "Gingflied" but he actually took up arms on the barricade in 1849. And those who are continuing these great artists works are the one who are fighting against capitalism of today. And I believe that they are the only ones who will be recognized as the greats artists in the future. Without grasping the stracture and tides of to-day's society, there can not be a great artist, this is my believe.

Sept. 17,

In front of the hotel where I stay, there are a big street cars barn, the union station and power house with more than a dozen of chimnies; and many a times I had impulse to paint this, but I have not any paints. I am wondering whether George would let me use his water colors. George and I are, of course, very good fried, but I don't know whether it is proper to ask him such a thing. If he is not using it at all, and if you think it is all right, Will you please ask him to lend me his a set of water-colors, and a pallet, and water-color and oil brushes two each? Would you do this for me?

Yesterday was an election of L.A., and we succeeded to recall mayor Shaw by a big majority, so much is good but an anti-picket ordinance was voted. We don't know sure, but in this fight it seems that businessmen have uper hand against labor. If this anti-picket ordinance becomes a law, we expect a wave of wage-cuts. So there are long fight ahead of us. We must fight always. Of course the world looks so dark, but there is always the sun beyond these dark clouds of war and injustice. World can keep out of war, if America did act. If this government of U.S.A. refuses to sell oil and iron to Japan, Italy and Germany, there will be no war in China and Spain, nor Germany could not make any truble in central Europe. I am against this war in China. I am helping Chinese to defeat the Japanese militalist's plots. This war is ruining not only Chinese cities and people, but also whole Japanese people, its home, its cultures. That why so many of Japanese are against this war. That is the why most briliant professors and writers were arrested and soldiers were shot in Japan. May be Japanese militalists will take Hankow or many other cities, but the final victory will be in the hands of the Chinese. And it'll not be far future that Japanese people will free themselves from the chains of the feudalism and the capitalism which caused this war. Don't be discouraged by this dark, rainy world situation. We will see, soon the beautiful clear sky and joyous sun. I like to say one word about the purges in Russia. It is not so bloody as the Hearst papers paint it. It is an act of selfdefence of Russian people, their home and the socialism for which they fought. All of those who were purged are murders, spies and ploters for the benefit of the facist countries, namely Germany, Japan, Italy, Poland and Great Britain. It was people of Russia who demanded death for these Polipical murders. There is no death sentences for ordinary murders.

Those who want to paint Russia as "bloody" is the one who want keep Tom Mooney in prison and who fight against anti-lynch law.

I better put down my pen or I could never finish.

Seattle will be colorful by this time. If you have time, go out and make sketches. I am sending you two booklets by Brawder, please read it so you will understand me more. By the way, I thank you sending my painting to the exhibition.

Good bye then

Yours truly
Shirō
Shiro Miyazaki

LETTER #22

From Shirō to Bill Gamble

577 S. Central St.
Oct. 29, 1938

Dear Bill:

I just don't know how to thank you. I think the best way to show you how much I appreciate your kindness is to send you some paintings which I am going to make.

But you should not send such new ones. I just wanted Georges old one, but new one is better.

I am certainly glad to hear the news of coming your marriage. I believes you two will make the happiest family. I wish I could be at your wedding but it is too far.

At the end of Sept. I attended a labor school of two weeks. There I learned such subject as the political economy, the economical American history, trade union movement and so force. There were all kinds of nationalities, Negros, Mexicans, Whites, and I, Japanese. We studied and played and lived just like brothers and sisters, it was just like heaven. I hope in the future we will have such heavenly society as I have had in that school. We called our school as "the little Soviet".

After I got through the school, I found a job just like George's and I am working almost Like George, from morning to late at night. I come back home after ten o'clock. What a world! There are millions who have no job to work and those who have a job much work such long hours just like a slave! We are tring very hard to solve this question through the labor union but it is not a easy job. Already two years passed after we started organizing this field.

Last Tuesday night which was my day-off, I went to hear the W.P.A. concert. They played Beethoven's 3rd (which is my favorit and R. Strauss' opus 40. They played so well! and yet there are so many mislead people who thinks that unemployed are good-for-nothing. Think of it!

Wish happiest wedding and thank you again the paint and palet and brushes.

Please give my regard to you future wife, Margaret.

Yours truly
Shirō Miyazaki

LETTER #23

From Shirō to Bill Gamble

L.A. Cal.
577 S. Central Ave.
Dec. 28, '38

Dear Mr. and Mrs. Bill Gamble:

On your wedding night, I have had a glass of cocktail for first time in my life. We drank it wishing your happiness.

Since the Thanksgiving I am working on a print which I'll call "Symphony of desert". Yesterday I took a proof of upper half. It is not so bad. As a fact, it is the best one I made so far. I hope I could send it to you by the new year. Then I am going to re-cut the Mt. Wilson, for the previous one has no poem and music in it. I hope I would make a success on it.

Did you see Lynd Ward's "Vertigo:. Lynd Ward is my tearch. I hope I'll get some lines from you during the vacation.

Wishing you a very marry Christmas, and a happy new year.

Yours very sincerely,
Shirō Miyazaki

Desert Symphony
(8" x 10")

Shiro made this block print from sketches he made when he was recuperating in Borrego Desert in San Diego County in May 1938.

LETTER #24

From Shirō to Bill George

Dear Geo. [Salutation is in English]

Your letter finally arrived.

Thank you. I'm glad. And for the money too. I know I shouldn't but I'm going to accept it. I used half of it as soon as I opened the letter. To explain, I worked only three days last week and didn't have the room rent, so I used it for that.

Recently, actually four or five days ago, I signed a contract to draw illustrations for a book on physiology for teenagers. The order is for a hundred and then there are about fifteen that I would like to include. For drawing the hundred twenty, it's fifty dollars. I don't know how long it will take, but in hours, it will be less than five cents per hour. But when I think it's the first step toward commercial drawing, it makes me happy. I'm going to do my best. The young man is also poor like me. Where I have a '28 Chevrolet, he has a '30 Packard. Although he is a doctor, he has an artistic temperament and is fun. The other day when I went to his home, his wife told me, "He's the kind of guy, when he went to the May Co. (a department store) to buy a pair of shoes, with that money he when and bought this book instead". Then she took from among four books on his desk, one thick book on Wagner's life and said, "He wanted to sell this for fifty cents. It's outrageous". I like him a lot, although I just met him. Therefore, I want to do a good job on the illustrations.

Also, the publisher is really high-toned, so if I do a good job, I may have a chance on the next one. I'm counting the chicken before they hatch!

One word on the desert picture. There is no feeling of a desert at all. A desert is nature in the nude! It's like an innocent child. It has the strength of a giant and the gracefulness of a woman. I can't, however, express that sort of feeling. To start with, this crazy capitalistic society that has outlive its time, has taken 'laughter' away from me. It has torn away joy. Like an aborigine in a primitive communistic village, I can't express the bright desert. As a technique, I used lino cut on the mountain and lino engraving on the sky and sand. Especially for the sand, I used this kind of engraving tools [a sketch of two types of tools are drawn]. At first I didn't think this type of tool would work on linoleum, but when I used it, it worked fine.

I want to continue going to school a little while longer to take up life drawing and portrait. I also want to work with clay. If I don't do this, I can't make a good block print. Still, I can't withdraw from the union activity for another year. I feel crushed. There's also this story about the guy who chased two rabbits.

Do you remember me smoking a lot? I quit from January 2nd. On the 2nd, while I was having lunch at a restaurant, they were playing Romeo and Juliet. Hearing that, I wanted a radio. When listening to a symphony, the body gets dignified and rhythm gets into the picture. So, if I quit smoking, I can save a dollar or a dollar and a half per week. That's why I quit.

Right now, when I'm looking at the desert print on the wall, the words Beethoven wrote on the notes of his third symphony, "Simple, simpler" came to mind. If I simplify it badly, the strength will be taken away.

Today, after I worked from eight in the morning until nine thirty at night (plus one and a half hours for travel), the leg I injured last year hurt.

Well then, just as a word of thanks.

[No address or date given, but believed to be January 1939 since a letter to Dr. Gamble dated January 9, 1939 had similar information of the illustration contract. The title of the book is, "Your Own True Story" by Berl ben Meyr was printed by the Caxton Printers, Ltd. Caldwell, Idaho in 1940. It had over 100 ink pen illustrations by Shiro.]

"Gas Storage Tank"

Linoleum Block Print
(7-1/2" x 9-1/2")

[I believe this tank was located just south of the Santa Ana Freeway, between Alameda Avenue and the Los Angeles River.]

LETTER #25

From Shirō to Bill Gamble

577 S. Central Ave.
Jan. 9, '39

Dear Bill:

I want you, you and George be the first ones to hear that I made a deal to make illustrations for a book. The book is "Your own true story" by Berl ben Meyr, a physiological book for ages 12 - 16, with over 100 illustrations. As far as the money is concern there is nothing to talk about. I'll get ten dollars when I submit all drawings, and I'll get 40 dollars when the authors royalty comes in, may be one or two years later; who knows? So he gave me liberty to choose style and so force of illustrations. I want to concentrate to this work about two or three months, then, may be, I may get some chances to go to some-where.

Did you get my print, the desert? I could not catch the feeling of desert, it is impossible for me to. Desert is nature in nude, bright and joyouce like the natives of primitive communistic village; how could I, who lies in the lower depth of dieing capitalism, express it?

Bill, you want to make money? I am going to make a calendar for 1940 with 12 lino-engravings. If you could sell it to a big concern for the price of 100 dollars, I will give you 50% of it. How about it? I was intending to write a long letter to you this time, but my eyes are tired already, I will write soon again.

Please give my best regard to your wife.

Yours very truly
Shirō Miyazaki

P.S. I typed it because it easier to read for you and easier for me to write.

[This letter was typewritten]

Letter #26

From Shirō to Bill Gamble

Jan. 11th, 1939
577 S. Central Ave.,
Los Angeles, Cal.

Dear Bill

The other night, I was listning to the fourth symphny of Tschaikowsky, and then came to me an idea how to finish the desert. I think I will finish it by three days then I will send you the prints, so please hold the prints if there are enough time for the north western print makers exhibition.

I made a drawing for a new print, called "zenith"; but I don't think I have the time for it. So please send the print of Mt. Wilson. By the way, please do not state them as lino-cut, but lino-engraving or just lino. Price? I don't care. It is up to you. Make it $1 or $100, any way no body is going to buy them. I am trying to sell my print for 25cents, but nobody cares for it. It is a sad world. And I hate to give it away to guys don't appreciate it at all. One of my print, a group of workers are longing to go home on the dock of Alaska cannery, which I made for the Shukaku, the Japanese literale magazine in which you gave the help with your prints, appeared in this week New Masses.

The work of illustration taking most of my time, and I can do nothing else until I finish it; so natually, the business of making calenda is out of question for a while.

If I have a little money, I would like to the desert and stay there one or two years studing drawing and print making from the great nature. Rodin says, "Where did I master Sculptur? In the woods, looking at trees on the roads, watching the structure of clouds; in the studio studing modeles, everywhere but in school"

I agree with him, though I am not going to say to you to quit your school, it is out of point.

You do not have to write answer for these letters I write. I am writing them, may be, I am lonely, no body to speak to, so I play with this typewriter.

From next week, I will attend a or two evening drawing class in De Vall Sculpture School in Hollywood, it cost me 50 cents per night and materials but I will manage some how

That all for to-night.

Yours truly
Schiro Miyazaki

P.S. Please forgive me not answering for all what you wrote in that long letter.

[This letter was type written.]

Letter #27

From Shirō to Bill Gamble

Dear Bill

You will hardly guess how gratefully I feel reciving your letter. Had I enough time, I would like to write an answer as long as yours. Last week I worked every day, and far bihind of the illustration works.

Your letter has so much meats in it that it is too hard to answer at once, so if this letter end short I will write some more in near future. First of all, I must thank you for kidnapping that lazy George for me. Do you know what I did with the ransom money he sent me? I paid my room rent with half of it, and with the other half I made a down payment for a radio which is now playing the Finlandia by Sibelius. Last night it brought me the Third symphony by Beethoven. Fine music gives me a kind of refreshment after a hard work of a day or during the drawing of illustrations.

Especially, I am grateful for your detailed criticisms of my print. Though I could see that you spent a great amount of time for it, I wish you will write some more when ever I send a print.

Why, yes Why didn't you send me the print of Mt. Shukan[9]? I like it. It is such a good work. I could learn lots out of it. It has what I haveN't. The simplicity, this is the thing I must learn from yours ann George's works "Simpler and more simple" Beethoven cryed. Back to the print, it has poem of, song of and power of the Northwestern and of the Rocky. Bill, you have a very good quality in you, please try to find it out and develope it. However I like to note one thing about the print. You speak of sacred quality of black of a print. Yes, it is important, but some times the black

---

9   Mt. Shukan should be Mt. Shuksan, a mountain in the Cascade Range, adjacent to Mt. Baker in northern Washington.

gives the feeling of emptiness, it hurt as much as over cut. See the left lower corner of the print, specially the trees. I try to cut every space of a block as I cover a canvas with paints, by doing so I think I could express more of reality. This is what I learned from my teach, Lynn Ward. Of couse, you don't have to cut in this way. There are thousands of ways to cut, and more must be created. In short I want to say is that the sacred black is just like opium which is very useful if it is used properly.

Now let us come back to my print, I mean the desert. All what you have said is true. I should write what I think of that print before. I did fall to show the distance of the plane,, not because the cut outs were too strong but the Ocotillo (read Ocotteya) was too thin and weak. By bringing Ocotillo out stronger I could be able to soften the contrast between the mountain and plane. So much for the technical matters, for you wrote me a great deal and I fully agree with you. It seems to me what wrong with the print lies in more fundamental thing. You see, the desert itself is nature in nude, it is powerful and joyous and open minded like a god. Or as I wrote to Geroge, the desert is the natives who lives in the vellage of a primitive communism and know no worries. But I who made the print live in the age of dieing capitalism that is fascism-war, wage cut and unemployes. (Incidentally, to-day we like Beethoven because he mirrored a dieing class that is fudalism and the riding class that is capitalism, as great artists always do. I will come back to this point later when I will touch in poems). This is the contradiction that appears in that print. May be I did not make it clear due to my poor English, then please guess what I want to say.

I am glad to hear that you are making poems seriously. I said making. I do same thing. I like poems which were made, and not scratched on a paper as inspirations spring out. May be you have heard or read that Edna St. Vincent Milley says, "Sometimes I work on a poem for a year, in my mind before I ever set in down on paper." I am glad you do the same. You are a real artist. I too take a long time to complate a poem mostly two or three months.

I would like read your poems soon, but please do not waste you time copying them for me. I am writing for the first issue of collection of your poems.

Although, I did not have a chance to read your poem, "Eagle Harbor, Bainbridge" in its entirety, judging from what you wrote me I like to say a thing or two. You know that most of Beethoven's symphonies end with glorious and victorious joys, though many of them start depressed even including a funeral march. This is because, in one hand, he himself had a very strong will power and pushed foreward and up breacking all difficulties that lies before him; on the other hand, he did speak through the music for the rising tide of the society of that time. It was the time that that social stracture was changing. The change do not take so smoothly, for ruling class will not give up their power so easily. So we saw the bloody strangle of French Revolution and American Civil War. And many a times, the rising tide were crushed by the ebb. Beethoven lived in that period and saw many things which depressed him so deep just as to-days world situation depress you, but Beethoven foresaw and believed in the final victory for the rising tide, that is the why his symphonys have the optimistic glorious ending.

I wish you will end that poem of yours in same manner as he did. Bill, civilization is not going to be ruined. Yes, I can see as you do the sad picture of the world. Yes, Austria and Sudetantland were lost and Spain is in very bad shape, thanks for Hitler and Mussolini and their stooges Chamerlain and Dadalier and the American Neutrality Act. But remmember that history itself repeat. Once Paris Commune was lost, but to-day France has republic. Yes, there were many a time that looked as fudalism crushed the rising capitalism complately, but what to-day we have? To-day we live in a age of changing of social stracture as Beethoven lived in; but this time it is from so called democracy to a higher democracy that is from class society to classless society. May it seem as fascism is getting upper hand. But they are doomed to pass away.

Bill, chase the cloud away from your head, then you'll see the SUN. Turn your eyes to the one sixth of the earth where a higher stage of civilization is making. Though most of people in that country do not believe in God, still they are realizing what Christ wished and die for. You do not have to look at the Soviet, look around of yourself. Tom Mooney was freed! Roosevelt is moving in to a right direction, I mean left. People are learning. From bitter experience of Chicago and Seattle, people of California learned the necessity of unity and elected progressive mayor and governer. In Los Angeles county, the same people who voted for and anti-picketing ordinance in the primary, casted their votes against same proposition two month later. You see how the people are learning.

As the dying fudalism needed Napoleon, to-day the so called democracy that is capitalism needs Hitler and Mussolini to crush the rising tide of people for real democracy. Remember the fate of Napoleon. And threw away your pessimism. It'll do not any good to you.

I wished you'd read the book I sent you 'The Peril of Fascism'. Because an artist, if he wished to be a real and great artist, must understand the straacture of the society in which he or she lives. I'll quote once again from Milley. She says, "a poet, certainly now, more that ever, must keep in touch with his time, must learn what people want to hear. But he must not try to write about these things until he has made them a part of the pattern. Otherwise his work is uncooked, undigested."

In the early summer of 1929, Stalin in his speech stated that a severe economical cricis will rock the United States soon, of couse economists in this country laughed at it, but what happen six month later is what you witnessed. This fact alone will be enough to prove how the Marxists way of annalicis is correct. And the Peril of Fascism" explains clearly the social stracture of this age for we can not understand what is fascism without knowing it. I wish you will read the book for your sake. To-day it is raining, but an artist should be able to look through the cloud into the sun. If you read that book, you will have more optimism, and work harder for it aim as God wished you, with your strong will.

Last night, I almost run over a lady. She was not hurt much. I took to her home and called a doctor. They were poor people. They said that their income is $40 a month and pay $20 for the rent. That is the why she said, "Purse, purse, my purse, where is my purse", as soon as I helped her up from the ground. She later explained that the rent for the next day was in that purse. Their family was so good nature family, and people who live in that poor hotel too were very kind to me. I was almost dried out touched by the warm human heart.

I think I better stop here, and send this letter out. I will write more answer later.

Yours,
Shirō Miyazaki

P.S. Three nights ago, first time in my life I saw the burning of a cross by KKK on a hill top.

After I wrote this letter I went to see the old lady I mentioned above. She was well and doing some house work. Both of us were lucky.

[Note: At the top of the letter '577 - S Central Ave.' and ' Feb 3' were penciled in.

Letter #28

From Shirō to Bill Gamble

Dear Bill

I just finished printing and going to send it to you.. Please do the all troubles of sending it to the exhibition. I printed six prints from the block. None of them is not so satisfactory. I guess if it was cut on wood, it would come out nicer.

Thanks for your poem.

I am glad you wrote such a giantic (sic) poem.

Wish this'll reach you in time.

I moved to 2805 W. 12th St. Los Angeles, Cal.

It is a quiet place.`

I'll write soon.

Shirō

[A notation of Feb 3 is on the letter]

LETTER #29

From Shirō to George

Hello Geo.

It must be lilac time in Seattle and life must be easier now. How is everyone?

This one-man exhibit you're putting up for me, I'm putting you through a lot of trouble. I leave it in your hands.

The other day, after I wrote to the school in San Francisco, they send back the watercolor painting I had left there. Please notify Bill of this too. I'll be painting a couple of watercolors soon, so when they're finished, I'll send them all together.

Now a days, I've been doing gardener's helper work. I was working four days a week at the market, but they became busy and asked me to work six days. If I worked six days, I wouldn't be able to do the illustrations, so I quit the market. Working four days as a gardener's helper, I'll have sufficient time for my illustrations and there'll be time in the evening, so when I finish with the illustrations, I'm thinking of learning drawing at night school.

One way or another, I want to exert my total effort toward art. Yet, just like you, I'm pressed to make a living. Which reminds me, how are you doing? You must also be busy making a living. But it's best not to drink too much now. At the end, drinking will overtake you and your artistic motivation will disappear. You have this artistic talent that I don't have. It's like, no matter how good the seed, it will rot if left alone. Talent alone is no good. You have to study too! Even Beethoven, even Rodin, even Cezanne studied until tears came. You can't get anywhere without motivation. This is what I need to tell myself too. Anyway, let's both pull ourself together.

Now and then I think I'd like to return to Seattle, but when I think I'm known as the undutiful son over there, there's no way I can go back. What a hard world to live in. By the way, send me a letter now and then. It's okay if it's simple. It's okay to just jot it down. What you are doing. How my papa, Shusaku or Jiunko are doing. Anything is okay.

I just returned from a meeting of a Japanese life insurance group recently organized around me, so I just picked up the pen for a moment before going to bed. Although it's life insurance, it's a mutual aid group and I don't get a penny out of it.

When the book I'm illustrating is published, I'll send you one too. It looks like it's going to be a good one. Just a short note.

Shirō

February 22ⁿᵈ

[Note: No address or year is given but believed to be 1939 and from his letter to Dr. Gamble writes that he moved to 2805 W. 12th Street, Los Angeles around February 3rd.]

Letter #30

From Shirō to Bill Gamble

April 3rd 1939

Dear Bill:

I offer you my congratulations. It made me happy and bright that you won the purchase prize in the Print Maker's Exhibition.

I always estimate highly that exhibition and it is a great honor to get a prize in it. Please keep up your good work. I know you will. I was thinking that if I do one more year of study in drawing, maybe it'll be possible for me to get one. I'll work hard and'll get a prize as you did, and may be three or four years later in "the Fifty Prints of the Year". This is my hope.

I suffered a stomach indigestion for past two days, so although I am all right now, I did not have enough energy to work on the illustrations. So I set this whole day as a real day, and I was reading Gorky's "The Specter", his last unfinished work, when mailman brought your letter.

The Specter is the fourth volume of Gorky's "Forty Years". I read the first volume, Bystander in Seattle nine years ago, The Magnet in San Francisco, and Other Fires in L.A. about two years ago, and every time finished the volume I looked forward for next volume, but now I cann't. This great artist have been murdered by the agent of Hitler. Speaking of Nazis, see that film "Professor Mamulock" by Frederick Wolf, by any means. It is a great masterpiece. After Wolf escaped from Germany he went to Austoria, there he wrote the play which were played on the stage of every country, of couse include not Germany and Italy, and then in Soviet he directed the production of the film. He is now in Paris. Set aside everything, and go to see this great picture, it'll move you and give you courage!

One more week, then I am going to lose my job. My boss want me to work six days a week instead of four days which I am doing now, more over, he wants me to move into his house which is near to the store, if I do so then I can not read anything I want to. and if I work six days a week I just can not work on the illustration at all. The illustration would not bring any money so to speack. But I can not just let him down.

And I think this is a good chance to change my occupation so that I can study in the evening.

My desert symphony is very very unpopular among my artist friends here. But I myself regard that print a important one for I found the pass of myself in that print. As soon as I finish the illustration work, though, I do not when, I'll made two prints, one is a locomotive repair shop with a strong contrast of black and white, the other will be a great big print of sky. I should say clouds expressing the feeling of suppressed anxiety and of hope.

I did not answer you long letter of last year in full. I'll do it some day. I can not do it now for I am somewhat restless.

I thank you for your kindness sending my prints and paintings to exhibition.

I hope you did go to that exhibition. May be you did yesterday that is April 2nd. If you did and if fine some time to spare, please write me your impression of that exhibition.

Yours very truly
Shirō

P.S. Of couse, please give my best regard to your wife and Geo.

And ask George to write to me about when he is coming to San Francisco to see the fair.

Letter #31

From Shirō to Bill Gamble

Dear Bill:

I don't know how to thank you doing so many things for me. I recived you letter about the one-man show, yesterday. Thank you Bill.

Have you got enough frames? It'll take a lots of times of yours and George's for which I am sorry.

After recieving your letter I wrote to the California School of Fine Art asking them to send me back my water-color of sunflowers which was mounted in a very good frame which cost me over seven dollars. I doubt whether they have them yet.

I'll paint two or three landscape water-colors. I can not say how it'll come out for I didn't touch the colors for years. But I feel shame to have a show with only 5 to 9 years old paintings.

Please tell me whether you are intending to include printings or is it all paintings. I'll leave the selections up to you and George.

I lost my job three days ago. It happened this way. I was working four days a week and on the off days I was doing the illustrations. But boss asked me to work six days a week. If I work six days a week fro early morning to late in the night I just have no time for illustration work, and I just can't turn the good natured author down. So here I am. A Jap without money. I am going to work as a gardener. Now I have two days work.

Thank you again

Yours truly
Shirō

LETTER #32

A postcard from Shirō to Bill Gamble

Shirō Miyazaki
2805 W. 12th St..
Los Angeles, Cal.

Mr. William Gamble
1902 - 8th West
Seattle, Wash.

Dear Bill:

Just one word to thank you for your kind letter.

Everytime I read your letter I feel that the best thing in the world
is a good friendship. You are all ways doing something for me, and
I never done even one thing to you - which I regret.

Yours truly
Shiro Shirō

[The postcard is stamped May 1, 1939]

[The post card has a photo of the Hollywood Bowl]

Letter #33

From Shirō to Bill Gamble

Dear Bill:

I don't know how to thank you, and I don't know how to apologize not writing sooner.

On last Monday the mailman brought your letter and found, with surprise and joy, the fifteen dollars in it. Without taking any chances, for I might use the money for something elso, I went to a store and bought 8 colors, four brushes, a half dozen of the Watmann, a canvas and its frame to stretch the water color paper on it, a port folio and a newly published Mosses' "Artistic Anatomy".

This annatomy book was a good bargain for I bought this bright new $3.50 book for $2.00 just because the corners of the cover was slightly damaged. Well, with your kindness, I got enough paints to last one or two years. Tomorrow -Sunday- I am going out to paint a hill on a canyon, and on the following Tuesday I will do some oil wells at Long Beach, and with one more and of course with the Sunflowers which I got from S.F. I will send them to you as soon as it possible, say 20th of this month.

But please do not expect any good ones for I can not gurantee them because I did not touch the water color paints about six years for one reason, and I am so busy now a days and so many things in my mind that I have barely have time even for sleeping. Some times I feel that f I do not became an insane, some thing is drastically wrong with me.

The illustration must be done at least with in one month, yet it seems to me I just started it. And in June 3rd we are going to have a big affair, called Anti-Fascist Japan NIght to raise money for our paper which is the only anti-war Japanese paper published in the

U.S. I am busying myself making posters for this affair for which we expect more that one thousand people to attend.

By the way, we got a donation of over twenty lithography and woodcuts for this affair. They are such fine prints that had I money I'll buy some of them.

Two of my friends are going to visit Seattle this summer, one in June and the other in July, though I wish I could go with them there is no possibility in sight. But they may see the exhibition.

Thanks for the list. Looking at it I could guess what hard time you and George have had. It is very kind of you spending so much of your busy time and energy for the exhibition.

After this busy time is over I will paint some thing very different from from previous work, something in that effect of the desert symphony which is very, very unpopular among my friends though. Although I myself do not know what in my mind but something different.

Thank you again, my best regard to Margaret.

Yours Truly
Shirō Miyazaki

[This letter was typewritten. No date or address is given; however, someone as penciled May 14]

LETTER #34

From Shirō to George

George thanks,

I received your letter and money last Monday. I should have sent you a reply right away, but it's been so busy these days, I can't do a thing.

I used all of the money you sent me for paint. Today, I'm took it and went to paint, but it's didn't go well. It was a terrific landscape but the adversary General is too complicated and I, myself, have forgotten how to paint with watercolor. To start with, I forgot how to mix the colors together. Then as I am painting timidly, the colors had an odd brightness and I wept. I finally finished with only a draft.

Today was a bad day. Leaving the house around 10 AM, on the way to a place about twenty miles away, the gasoline fuel line clogged. Puttering around, it was three o'clock before I started painting. To top it off, it was in a no smoking area and to boot, I couldn't stand the cold. I gave up after painting about an hour. This Tuesday, I'll go there again or should I go to Long Beach to paint the oil derricks? As to whether I can come up with one that I can put in an exhibit, I don't have the confidence. For places I want to paint, there are plenty.

In a month or two, I'll be through being busy, so I intend to start working on the foundation of art. For that and in remembrance of the money you sent me, I bought a book on anatomy. It's a very good book! Along with that, when I get the time, I think I'm going to join the American Artists Congress so I can establish a rapport with the Caucasian artists. To me, I feel I can absorb art best if I go back to Seattle where both you and Bill are; but, as you know I'm known as the unfilial bad boy so I can't return.

By the way, recently I've been so completely tired, I feel just like a mechanical robot. Since there are so many different things I have to do, tolerating a four-day income of ten dollars and change and with hardly any time for play, I am pressed with work. These days, I really think I should never have accepted that illustration job. Looking from a socialistic viewpoint, they're all worthwhile but then it's awful to be chased around for a debt on a shirt. Honestly, at times, I think it's much easier to go crazy.

Saying it's disgusting to live in a society that sets the value of a man's worth by his monetary holdings, other than grin and bear it, there is no other way. Therefore, although Bill wrote asking me to persuade you to study art, I can't get in the mindset to tell you to become an artist. Saying that, I myself hate a life where you work only for money and nothing else even more. I don't know why I'm writing this sort of thing.

I'm going to be obligated to you for this up coming exhibit. The artwork I have here, I'll send them by the 20th or the 22nd. If I can do that, there should be time.

Two of my friends are going to Seattle in June and July, so please show them where the exhibit is at that time. Also, if it's all right with you, when they return, why don't you ride down with them in their car, take in the fair in San Francisco and then come down here. If you come during the summer, we can go to the Hollywood Bowl together and listen to the symphony.

Well. I'll excuse myself now. Thanks. Write to me again.

Shirō

[No address or date. Presumed to be in Los Angeles and possibly written in mid May 1939 as similar reference of two friends going to the Seattle in June and July were included to his letter to Dr. Gamble, where Dr. Gamble had penciled in May 14th.]

LETTER #35

From Shirō to Bill Gamble

May 18th, 1939

Dear Bill:

Thank you, thank you. I don't know what to say. This five dollars is not a five dollars for I can not set the value of your friendship in dollar and cent.

Your letter was waiting for me when I came back home from the oil field where I was painting a hill and oil wells. I'll finish it on coming Sunday. Here I have one which I have painted on last Sunday and Tuesday. With the sunflower I'll send you three paintings altogether on Monday or Tuesday (22nd or 23rd).

The nature is so beautiful, but my paintings are all dull, just like my head and this man made society. I guess if this society was changed so that it'll grow as natural, then my paintings too will become more beautiful. On this subject, the other day I heard very good speech on Thos. Mann over the radio which was deliveried at the International Writers Congress in the New York World Fair. If I could hold a copy of that speech I'll send it to you.

One before last time when George sent me five dollars I spent half of it for down payment of a radio and the half for my room rent! Since then it was bothering my conscience, that is the why I spent the 15 dollars for art materials. The money you sent me is a great help for me, but please do not send me any more. Today I went to see the All California Exhibition and read a note on an artists whose income was five dollars a week and out of this he paid one dollar for drawing -class, and yet he kept on his study. I should be doing same thing but I am so lose on money. I wish I have a strong will power like him.

I guess you've had a hard time selecting from small amount of my painting for "your exhibition". I hardly could call it "our exhibition" for I did not do anything, all were done by you and George. Without your kindly help I would not be painting to-day. I leave all it up to you. If you want some particular painting to keep at your home or George's, you could put sign of the N.F.S. Although there'll be one out of one thousand chances that we may sell even one. By the way, if it is all right with you and George I like to ask you to arrange the exhibition at the Chinese Artists Club and we could send the money to the Chinese medical aid for the victim of the war. "Japanese help Chinese" with this headline, if we had good publicity in the Commonwealth newspaper, P.I. and others, we may sell some, then we could give 2/3 or 3/4 of the sall to Chinese and lest of them to you. You should get some for the all works you have done.

You see, although I was not responsible and was against from the start to this war in China, but since I am a Japanese I feel a kind of guilty myself. That is the why I am asking you this so that I can clear my conscience a little.

But if it bothers you or George, let us drop this idea.

It is (a diagram of a clock face with the hands pointing to one - forty five) now, so taking your advise I'll say good-night.

Yours truly
Shirō

LETTER #36

A postal card from Shirō to Bill Gamble

Shirō Miyazaki
648 Stamford Ave.
Los Angeles, Cal.

Mr. William Gamble
1902 - 8th West
Seattle, Wash.

Dear Bill:

I am on the road again with my suitcases.

This time I moved to Room 310 - 648 Stamford Ave., Los Anglees

I am sending you a lino-cut. This was made for a poster. The subject is a colored lady, natoinaly known figure. How is the our exhibition? I always feel grateful to you

Yours
Shirō

[The postal card is date stamped May 20, 1939]

LETTER #37

From S Shirō to Bill Gamble

May 23rd, 1939

Bill:

I just finished the packing of painting. I am going send it to you this afternoon. When you open it, you too will disappointed as I am. Best thing in that package is the frame. I just forgot how to paint water-color, more over I am so tired that there is no fire in me burning to paint. I could promise you that after this busy time is over I'll paint some for the fall northwestern show.

The two paintings is not as good, especially the oil wells. I wish you don't show it in out show.

I put "the Progressive Weekly" in between the two paintings, on the page six of it, you'll find a copy of Mann's speech at the Pen Club. He talked over the radio with such feeling that his voice is still ringing in me. Isn't it the time lilac and horse-chestnuts bloosom in Seattle?

Excuse me with this short note and bad writing.

Yours true friend
Shirō

Letter #38

A postal card from Shirō to Bill Gamble

648 Stamford Ave.
Los Angeles Cal.

Mr. William Gamble
1902 - 8th West
Seattle, Wash.
June 1st

Dear Bill:

Please do me a favor, that is, if we are going to have a catalogue for our exhibition, send a copy of it to Miss Brown, art teacher in care of Garfield High School in Seattle, although I do not know whether she is in that school or not. I owe her lots in the study of painting.

Yours very truly
Shirō Miyazaki

LETTER #39

From Shirō to Bill Gamble

June 8th, 1939

Dear Bill:

Drop me a note. You don't have to write a long one. I know that you were busy and yet busy for you piled your own works preparing for my show. Just drop me a note about how you are getting alone, for I am afried of that you might get sick working to hard for the show.

I could breath a little easier for we are through with the affair which I wrote you before. Many people, more than we expected, came to the Anti-fascist Japan night, and we made a lots of money for our paper.

During last two weeks I worked only two days, and on the last of days, I steped on the gass in order to bring the illustration to the finish line. Unfortunately I could not finish them.. There are some more to do -- and I am tired out.

From coming Monday I am going to work in a fruits and vegetable stand. This job was offered to me weeks ago, but I just could not take it for my hands were tide up with the illustration. Since the end of the illustration is in sight and I must do something in order to eat, I am going to take it. This is much better job than I have had in Japanese fruit and vegetable store, for it is a A.F.of L. union store, therefore working hour is shorter and wage is higher and best of all I could go to an evening class. You see I want to take up drawing or scaluptur as soon as I get through with that illustrations.

The other day at public libraly, I was looking through 'The Mad man's drum', and an idea of a cut for your Heritage come to my mind. I thought I don't know wheather I can master it or not, nor do I have clear understanding on you poem, Heritage.

I am reading Malraux's "Man's Hope" which I borrowed from a public libraly. I heard him speak in Los Angeles about two years ago and have read his Royal Road, yet I did not know until this time that he is such a great writer that I do not hesitate to call him one of the greatest writer of our day.

George drinks too much, and I smoke too much. I wish I could have the will power of yours.

By the way, let us drope the idea of having the exhibition in Japanese C.C. or Chinese Art Club. It is too much trouble. I think you better put that time in your work.

Please accept my many thanks for what you have done and doing for that exhibition, and the prints which I am going to send you, one for you and one for George.

The print were made and given by George Welner whose name will become known in the future. He is about my age and works in a printing shop in which we print our paper.

Please give my best regard to your Margaret.

Yours truly
Shirō

P.S.

PLease tell george I'll write him soon. You said he is a great guy, I agree with you 100%

LETTER #40

A postcard from Shirō to Bill Gamble

>Mr. Bill Gamble
>1902 - 8th West
>Seattle, Wash.

Dear Bill:

This is where I have been today. Two days ago one of us got fired, so all of us got out of the camp.

I'll write you as soon as I have new address.

Yours truly
Shirō

[The postcard is stamped June 9, 1939 and postmarked San Francisco]

[The post card has a photo of a statue Evening Star - Court of Honor, Golden Gate International Exposition '39]

LETTER #41

From Shiro to Bill Gamble

> June 26
> 648 Stanford Ave.
> L,A, Calif.

Dear Bill:

Thanks for you letter. I feel grateful to you writing to me. I was worring not hearing from you, then it was George who kept your letter for a whole week; but let us excuse him this time for he sent it with "Special Delivery - Air Mail" stamp on, and with his own long letter. Thanks again for let him write to me.

I must do some more drawings for illustration before I go to bed, so please excuse me with following short notes:

I am glad your school is out and could do gardening and other house work.

I am sorry I can not tell you anything about the Art Center School right now, I'll find out as soon as possible and write to you.

What you said about benifit show for the Chinese is just what I was thinking when I wrote you asking to forget what I wrote in previous letter about this business.

George wrote to me that he enjoyed the Sunday drive you had with him. He is too lazy to go out alone, so if you ask him to take you and your Margaret to, say, Ranier Mt. [Mt. Rainier] it'll help him to bring back what he was used to.

Bill, you are a natural born Communist! This is what I felt when I read your letter which says, "What does it matter whether you or I produce it". There are not many even in the rank of Communist party members who are so great as you are. It takes long time to change one's character.

Do you remember you wrote me your future plan including the plan to study the Japanese art in Japan? I wanted to write answer for a long time but I cann't yet. In short I can say this that it is not wise thing to do, that is to study old Japanese art. If you try to apply the old Japanese art to your design or painting or prints, you'll get funny or pitiful result, something like the swing version of "Volga Boat Song" which I heard the other day over the radio. The most of Japanese art is the product of feudalism. You can not apply it to our art. Best thing to do is to learn from the nature (including our society) in which we live. It is not easy task, but I can not see any other way. To explain fully what I wrote above I should write a long article for which I have not time now.

Bill: give me more of your analysis on my painting. I think I am sientifically minded to recieve it. But not of that stuff called "praise". I expect more severer criticisms.

I want to destroy that "Montebello oil wells", have I had time to paint another one.

By the way, tell me what others are saying about the one man show, and please send me if there were any newspaper criticisms of our show. I like to see them.

Bill: you cann't and should not speak of Van Gogh in same rank with me.

He is such a great artist that you can hardly find one in 100 years. Who would paint a waste of land like he did?

Only regret is that he was born too soon. Had he lived to-day, he would not painted so madly but more constractively, may be he would not have died that way. For to-day we could have real hope. For we are going to finish the preface of human history and into the Chapter I where we can call ourselves really human beings.

Or in the other way, if I lived in the age of Van Gogh lived in without knowing Marx, I'll be lieing beneath the root of grasses it not become insane. So much for that.

Well it is about time to go to bed. I must get up 4:30 am. L.A. is so large, too large, and I must go 12 miles to go to work.

I wanted to write to George tonight, but let it go for tomorrow.

Yours truly
Shirō Miyazaki

LETTER #42

From Shirō to George

George,

Should you have on hand some money you don't have an urgent need for, can you send me twenty dollars? I want to go to night school, but I'm all empty. To amass twenty dollars will take me four weeks and I can't wait. I don't think I can return it in a hurry either, because I have some debt.

If there are any buyers, it's okay to sell my works at whatever price and you can and take it out from there. From now on, I plan to make them ten times better and draw by the hundreds, so isn't it better to sell them fast and sell them all?

If there is no buyer, I'll have the young man send you direct from my illustration money. Of course, this money will come next year only after the book is published and sold. I'm sorry, it's always the same thing but if you can, please send it.

Right now, I am on my way home from work and am writing this letter from the post office.

How's your health? I've had this cold for over two week and having a rough time. Sunday, which is day after tomorrow, I plan to finish the watercolor I had started. When I'm finished, I'll send it.

Well, I'm depending on you.
Shirō

[No address or date given]

Letter #43

From Shirō to George

George,

It's difficult for me to say this, but can you send me ten dollars. I'll return it as soon as I get my money from the illustrations. To tell the truth, I don't have the money to buy paint for the exhibit paintings. It's hard for me to ask this, on top of the paint you and Bill had sent. Right now, my weekly income is only ten dollars, and I'm barely able to eat. Here, although they'll lend me money to buy a battery for my car, I have no friend who will lend me money to buy such extravagant things as art paint.

Of the paint both of you sent me, I need to replenish seven colors as well as a few brushes, so please.

As I had not done any pen drawing, I was wondering how it would turn out, but it looks like I'll be able to go ahead with the illustrations in good order. The only problem is that it takes so much time.

I have been racking my brains for two weeks now about this money problem. Bill's letter arrived yesterday and after reading it, I made up my mind to ask you. Concerning the exhibit, I'm going to ask you and Bill to handle everything. Although it's a lot of trouble, can you make a list of which works will be exhibited and send me the list?

This is just a short note for the above urgent request. I'll write a detailed letter later. Take care of yourself and regards to all.

Shirō

[No address or date given]

LETTER #44

From Shirō to Bill Gamble

August 6th, 1939

Dear Bill:

Tegami to shashin to newspaper no clippings o okutte kerete arigato. (Thank you for sending the letter, photographs and newspaper clippings.)

Well, I better switch from Japanese to English for Japanese is not so popular since the war in China started.

Seeing the photographs which you sent me, I should say that the framing of our show are masterpieces. Seldom we see such a unified show are you arranged.

I feel a little freer for at last I finished the illustrations. I finished it last Sunday night, but I was so tired out from the strain of the continuous work that I could not do anything during last week except go to work for my daily bread and come back and read a book laying on the bed. Best part of all these excitements of last six or seven months is that I received six dollars so far.

The same author has a novel which he sold to a publisher and asked me to make about ten chapter-heads in lino-cuts but I did refuse it on the pretext of having no time.

Of couse I did waste enough time and this is the time to start for my drawing study in evening class. But real reason of my refusal is that the content of the novel is kind of reactionally stuff though he himself thinks that he is a progressive. If you read Gorky's the Spector (fourth volume of the Fourty Years) there you have a good picture of the said author in that Clism Samgin (the main character of the Fourty Years)

I don't want to share the dishonor with him.

The book I read last week is a biography of Tchaikovsky in which I found an amazing coincidence. In a letter Tchaikovsky wrote to Mme Von Meck, his financial supporter perhaps mentally too, the attitude of composing his fourth symphony. It was same process I took in engraving "the desert symphony". I think I wrote you before that I got the feeling or inspiration for that print from the 4th. I am thinking that would not be it better if we call the print, "Tchaikovsky's Fourth Symphoney" or "Tchaikovsky on the desert" instead of the "desert symphony". What do you think? Have you any better title for it?

There are so much in common between engraving and symphony. The other day I heard Liszt's Faust, and it's first movement just fit to a print which I have had in my mind since last winter. I'll start on this engraving as soon as I finished following preparation.

a. study of winter clouds which is main subject.
b. some sketches of sky-line of a small town.
c. purchase a big block of box-wood. I want do it on a wood for first time and big one too.
    May be I better do some practice on a small wood.
d. if possible to listen to the Liszt's Faust first movement by finding out someone who have the records or by purchasing the records and record player myself.

I think I'll finish this print by the time of next North-western Prints Show. By the way I have great admiration for its high standard of quality of the N.W. Print Show (though not of paintings)

Concerning to that exhibition in Chicago, it'll be a good idea if we send some of ours, yours, George's and mine. It is impossible for me to make new one by Sept. 30th so let send the desert print. Please do not send any other for I don't think that I have any other which is good enough for the exhibition.

Piccaso's painting which he have done in 1937 are coming to Hollywood soon.

This exhibition was brought here by the Hollywood Motion Picture Artist Committee and is going to charge admission in order to raise money for Spanish refugees for whom Piccaso too is helping.

Hollywood is an interesting town. Take the members of said committee, they are top-ranking directors, screen writers, actors and actoress. And those who get thousands dollars a week are members of C.I.O. and fight for progress and peace and against barbarous distractions of fascism shoulder to shoulder with those who get ten or twenty dollars a week. They became so progressive that even Shirley Temple is a communist according to the report of that Dies' Committee.

The Piccaso's exhibition particularly interest me, for some time I am thinking to find out some way to combine the realism of early Renaissance that is of 15th centure and the abstraction of post-war period of twenty century in order to express our emotion which we recieve from our socieal life and what is happening in the world today. This Piccaso's exhibition will give me some idea to that print.

Tell me what day is the last day to enter for the NorthWestern exhibition. I may send so water-colors if there are enough time for it.

Please give my best regard to your Margaret.

Yours truly
Shirō

P.S. Sorry I did not get any information about the art school to which your brother is going to attend.

LETTER #45

From Shirō to George

Hello George,

I finally finished the illustrations. After seven months, it feels like a load has been lifted off my shoulders. The pep has been drained out of me, so I didn't do a thing last week. Talking about doing things, reading Tchaikowsky's biography was about all I did. This week too, I plan to rest and read some more at night. I borrowed Aline Kistler's "Understanding Prints", published by the Associated American Artists, from the library and is a very good book.

From next week, I'm thinking of going to night school somewhere and try to learn drawing for about four nights a week.

Thanks for the photos of the exhibit. When I line them up and paste them in an album, it's like going to a museum. I was amazed at how well the framing was done. You must have really busted your back.

Yesterday I wrote to Bill but since English was my weak point in middle school where I received only E's and F's, I kept putting off the letter; however, among the pictures in the exhibit, the still life with the white border, the still life with the carrots, the landscape you drew when you and Sadao went matsutake mushroom hunting, aren't these pieces without value for an exhibition?

Right now, I'm listening to to a radio program from Portland that is broadcasting Beethoven. I sure would like to make a masterpiece like this. In art, of course, not music. I write a lot about music, but even now, I don't understand do, re, mi, fa..... Do you remember when we were sitting with our legs crossed at Shima's strawberry farm and you were trying to teach me do-re-mi? If I could understand music and not just feel it, how much better it would be! I'm thinking of going to Hollywood Bowl this Friday as I haven't been there once this season. To gaze at the moon, watch the stars while listening to the symphony and the sounds of the summer insects at the Bowl is the best thing for resting body and soul.

By the way, why don't you get married and settle down if there is someone good? If you do that, won't that decrease the number of sake cups? How about that, instead of art? Isn't there anyone? Saying this, it's funny, here I am with less artistic talent than you trying to become an artist, but for me, there's no one to marry. It's a world where without 'thirty pieces of silver', no girl will ever look your way. A little while ago, I did some calculating and found that since the time I was laid up by the accident, I have about seventy five dollars of debt that I have to pay back. I'll have to get the car overhauled pretty soon and then I'll need another twenty dollars. Of course, what I owe you or what I need to replace my worn out shoes and shirt, are not included in the calculation. God damn! When I think of money, my head gets heavy. That's why I guess the sky in that block print of the desert must also be so heavy. However, they say that good art and poverty always go together, so that must mean I have one of the qualifications for becoming a good artist. Yet poverty is nothing to admire. There's this kind of a story: Berlioz dreamt of a symphony one night. After he awoke, he went to his desk and started to write but then, "Wait a minute. If I write this section, I'll probably write it to completion. Then I won't be able to do anything else for four or five months but exert all my effort in this. With my wife ill and with no income, what shall I do? After I finish the symphony, I'll be so tired I'll have to have someone copy it for me. Then to compensate, I'll have to borrow. When the copying is done, I'll want to have it played. To have a concert, the income will be only half of the expense. Then I shall lose what I don't have. I shall want the necessaries of life for my poor invalid and shall have no money for myself." He thought to himself and decided to forget about the symphony. Berlioz then writes, "I hardened myself against temptation. I clung to the hope of forgetting - - -. Finally, all recollection had vanished forever."

So, if you had money, you would have become a famous artist by now. When it gets like this, poverty is not worth praising.

Even when I was jobless, I somehow had enough to buy cigarettes, yet when I'm working I still have only enough for cigarettes. I don't understand this world.

I intend to make one good block print by this winter. And I'm going to carve it in wood. Since I already have the mood of the picture in my mind, it should turn out to be the best one I ever made. Wait for it. On this point, I already wrote to Bill about it, so I'm not going to repeat it here. To begin with, there's no time. I have to get up early in the morning (before five o'clock), so I'm going to bed although I still have more things to write about. If I leave it until tomorrow, this letter might end up lying on this desk for a week like the other letter.

As usual, all I wrote about was money but this is always stuck in my head and it's only to show the contradiction of this society, not to ask you to send some more money. In fact, when you do send it, it's painful to me, so please don't send any. As long as I work, I'll get by.

Write to me once in a while about the people over there. Till then.

Shirō

August 7th

[Address and year is not provided]

LETTER #46

From Shirō to Bill Gamble

Aug 7th, 1939

Dear Bill:

Excuse me with this short note for I just come back from a Japanese writers and artists meeting, and 12 p.m. mover I got get up by 4:30 am. so have not time to write long letter.

In that meeting I learned that the Art Center School a kind of commercial art school - not for creative art, and they recomended the photographic classes very favorbly.

Truly yours
Shirō

P.S. Today I started for a drawing which will be down by water-color later, I don't know hot long it'll take.

LETTER #47

From Shirō Shiro to Bill Gamble

I found this letter un-mailed, so I am enclosing with others

Sept. 9, 1939

Dear Bill:

Last week, I recieved your letter which I think you wrote one month ago.

It was very good of you writing to me such a painstaking letter, rather criticisms to my paintings. It did surprise me that you have understand my feelings which I have had when I painted them.. I want to write an answer to the questions which you raised in the letter at great length, but haven't got time to do so.

The other thing I wanted to thank you is that, through you efort, George started to write me letters. Last time one was as long as eight pages!

The other night I saw Picasso's Guernica. I never saw such a strong mural painting before. Picasso is changing not only on his subject of painting but also in the form of painting. He will chang some more if he walks same way which he took last three or four years.

In that mural I could not see any trace of pessimism which we saw in his early paintings. I think this was due to the fact he grasped the "man's hope" through the participation in the formation of Popular Front and Spanish civil war.

There were many drawings which he worked as studies for the mural. Especially interested me were lines which connect eyes and mouth. I think these lines represent nerves. The mural was done in black and white, may be he intended to finish in color for

I saw a few of the drawings for this mural were colored. So much for Picasse.

I started for a water color, but found out that it is impossible to paint without a model. I have a lino-block (8" x 10") on which I draw a locomotive. I'll try to finish this by middle of September.

Sorry I haven't time to write any more to-day.

Yours very truly
Shirō

LETTER #48

From Shirō to Bill Gamble

Sept. 9, 1939

Dear Bill:

Since I recieved your long letter about three weeks ago, though you wrote them two months ago, I was saying to myself "I'll write it tomorrow, I'll write it tomorrow". But seems to me there'll never comes the tomorrow.

It was very kind of you that you look very deep into my paintings. It seems to me you know all of my feelings which I have had when I painted them.

Bill: at last, I made up my mind about myself. I am going to be an artist! Van Gogh started at thirty years of his age; I am twenty-nine, so it'll not be to late to start. I'll start from drawings from life.

On last labor day, I started on a water-color. I'll finish it on this coming Sunday. There is something good quality in it. I did not notice it before. I'll send it to you when I finished it.

What is happening inside of me, I don't know. I can not enjoy symphony, and found myself reading novels when ever I have the chance. Read recently: Gorky's short stories, The grapes of Wrath and Lust for Life (a novel based on the life of Van Gogh)

I wrote this short note to let you know that I am still living: I hope I can get up early Sunday so that I can have a time to write to you some more

Yours very truly

Shirō

LETTER #49

From Shirō Shiro to George

[First page is missing]

No matter, your working hours are too long. At the market where I work, there are more than twenty five working in the vegetable and fruit section, but the manager comes at seven in the morning and leaves at six in the evening. Yet, at your store there's no reason why you have to work from morning until late at night. There's nothing to hesitate about. Youth won't come around the second time, so talk to your mother. If you don't, I'll write a letter (of course, with your permission).

I want to go back and return to Seattle. After I pay back my debts and if I have about a hundred dollars for living until I find work, I may return, since there's no need to live with my old man. What I need are friends like you. I hear you're planning an exhibit in Japanese town of me. If someone has to go and keep watch, I think it's better not to have it. It's just a waste of time. However, if you do do it, I'm going to leave every up to you people. If possible I would like you to leave only the "Picture of Yesler Way" and the oil painting I did when we went out together in May. If perhaps, you can get quite a bit for them, I won't mind if you sell these too. The two "Sunflowers" belong to you guys, so it's NFS. (Not For Sale)

For those people who want my pictures, you should sell it to them according to their pocketbook. If the person want it to use as decoration to add weight to his house or wants the picture because he likes it and not because of his friendship with my father, it's okay to sell it to him at the price he wants to pay. For guys like you or Bill who try to understand me, it's an honor if you would take it for free.

Last Sunday, I started painting in watercolor, but without a model it's useless. I gave up and quit. Right now, I'm drawing a locomotive engine on an 8" x 10" lino block, but I don't know when I'll finish it.

Three evenings ago, I went to see an exhibit of Picasso's mural "Guernica" with about thirty draft drawings. It's a splendid piece of work. Picasso is changing. The painting was powerful, like dynamite.

Today I went and saw "They shall have music". I went in at one thirty in the afternoon and when I can out, it was six o'clock. I saw it twice. I'll probably go see it one or two more times.

Good news: Someone went and stole my rattly old car for me. I'm thankful to that thief. If I have it, I don't feel like selling it because of the convenience, but with it, it was a source for headaches. I guess no one can understand the feeling, unless he has such a junk. Should I use this as the theme for a short novel, I may be able to come up with a Gorky.

I have the photo of the oil you painted. Focus the camera when you take the pictures. Also, can you somehow take and send me a photo of my mother's portrait I painted? If you're able to take it, will you send me the negative? Or else, will you send me a 5" x 7" enlargement print?

This is a figgity letter but please excuse it.

My regards to everyone. I intend writing Bill a long one some day. Excuse the scribbling.

Shirō

[No date or address, however, it is believed to be written in September 1939 as the reference to Piccaso's ' Guernica' is similar to that in his letter to Dr. Gamble of September 9, 1939.

I remember and can see in my mind's eye the beautiful portrait Shirō painted of my mother using a photograph as his model. I often wondered whatever happened to it and wishfully hoped that I could find it and buy it from whoever owned it.]

LETTER #50

From Shirō to Bill Gamble

Sept. 12

Dear Bill:

It is raining. I can hear it. The rain and symphony from radio mixed together, and I was reading the heated arguments between Van Gogh and Gaugin in the Lust for Life.

The footsteps of the rain brought me to Seattle and thus I started to write to you this letter.

Today, from street car I saw a sun set. I never saw such a beautiful, powerful and emotional sun set before: I guess my artist is coming back. I'll paint the sunset next Sunday.

Yesterday, I finished a water color which I began on the Labor day. -- I'll send it to you two or three days later. You see. I want to keep it for a while and study it.

I feel it was a failure, yet there are good points too. Before I write you about them, I want to hear from you. Please write me after you recieve the water-color.

If you feel it is good enough to send it to the North Western show, please do the trouble of sending it to the show.

I am listening to Beethoven's fifth --

The water-color is the same size with the two, I sent previously, therefore there'll not be much trouble of framing it.

I am thinking that after I attended life class for half year, I like to go to the country and concentrate to study of painting, I don't know how long. A friend of mine lives in Mountain View, near

San Francisco, it he acept me I can paint there, working part time on his ranch. I want to begin the study of painting from bare earth --- naked nature --- though I could feel power of the earth on the pavement in the city street.

Excuse me writing in pencil, it is easier for my to write and with pen, I can not put down my thoughts so freely as with pencil.

Shirō

[Dr. Gamble noted: Post marked Inglewood, Calif. I had to send postage for W.S.G.]

LETTER #51

From Shirō to George

George

Speak of the devil and he appears. I wrote about unemployment and before I had a chance to send the letter, I became unemployed.

This morning, when I went to the store, everything from sugar to oranges was burnt black from last night's fire. And my job was burned out too. So now, I have to find another job, but as I want to find a job where I can go at least to night school without being rushed, I'm going to borrow the money you sent me to use as living expense. I know you didn't send the money for that purpose, but I used last week's wages for tuition and because I don't know when it'll be for this week's because of the fire.

This is just a short note. I'm going to school now. This evening, it's quick sketches. 'Til then.

Shirō

[No date or address but based on the following letter the year has been determined to be 1939.]

Letter #52

From Shirō to George

Hello George

Southern California is terribly hot! Still, because of this heat, I was able to get rid of the cold that had me racking with cough and phlegm. To tell the truth, I was worried that I might have caught pneumonia, but now I'm well.

Since the fire at the store, I'm taking a vacation with the money you sent me and not looking for work. It's not that I'm being lazy. For no reason, the muscles of the fingers and palm of my right hand hurt as if they're going to come apart and is very hot. Just then I became unemployed, so I decided that this was a good opportunity to recuperate. It still hurts when I carry heavy things but I'm thinking of looking for work from next week. I'm sorry to have spent your money like this.

It is really hot! I can't even go out to sketch. So, yesterday I painted a watercolor from the window. It took from six thirty in the morning to past one in the afternoon to finish painting it. The result was, it turned out to be such a hot picture, I just hated to look at it. And then, I can't get the thickness of the brick wall of the hotel on the other side to show up. I'm thinking of drawing it over again tomorrow.

The nude drawn in this letter was copied from those I did last night in the five minute sketch class. She was a splendid model. I have a fanciful ambition of hiring a model like this and do a life-size oil painting in a pose of my choosing.

School is three nights a week, with quick sketch one night while the other two nights are spent with those who are painting in another class. As the last two weeks were of the same pose of a person with a veil over her head and looked like a gypsy, I am disgusted. The quick sketch class, though, is a lot of fun. Since I have paid my tuition for two weeks, I should be able to find work within that time and continue somehow.

This morning I worked on the block prints that I had left alone for quite a spell. In the afternoon, I plan to do a self-portrait drawing.

At this autumn exhibit coming up, after a long spell, your work will be shown at last. Be sure to take pictures and send them to me.

Are you still on the water wagon? When you feel you want to drink, force yourself to paint and fake it. Just grab anyone, it doesn't matter whom and have him sit, then draw. Also, see a movie once in a while. There are some good ones. I think "They shall have music", "Golden Boy" and "Fifth Avenue Girl" are all worth seeing.

Will write again. Write to me too when you feel inclined.

Shirō

[No date or address but is from Los Angeles and believed to have been written in 1939 based on the movies which were all produced in 1939, The painting he writes about, he called it "The Back Yard".]

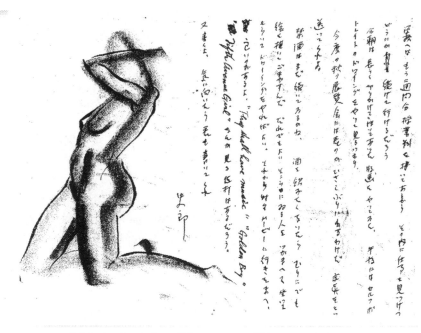

This is the 3ʳᵈ and last page of Letter #52.
Shirō liked to sketch on the side of his letters.

LETTER #53

From Shirō to Bill Gamble

Sept. 18th, 1939

Dear Bill:

It is too hot to sleep. The paper says that L.A. did not have such a heat for past quarter of century. Any way it is such that more I peel off, I get hoter. What do I peel off --- coat, pants, shirts, so force ---. One thing good about this heat is that it took away my cold which I have had for three weeks.

I just came back from the evening school at where I have been struggling past two and half hours over a girl's head. The propotion gone off track. Of couse, it is not only in my drawing that I don't get propotion right, but in everything I do, the way I live and the way I look at life --- may be ----.

But I can't ---- and must not let it go. I must master correct propotions in my drawings. If I could not correctly (that is in propotion), how could I apply the abstraction freely! or powerfully? Since I can not get model to work on except three nights a week, I do some copying from Michel Angelo or old Italian masters. I know that one drawing from life is better than ten copyings, but they are better than doing nothing.

I would like, if I could, to join the art project in W.P.A. for two reasons. One is that I could live doing the work as an artist, and the other is that I want to paint collectively as some of them are doing for murals.

The other day I saw the exhibition of works of Southern California division of W.P.A. Art Projects. It was one of best exhibitions I have ever seen. But -- yes But, unfortunately I was born in Japan, and orientals whose were not born in this country are not given the right to become American citizens, and W.P.A. enroll only American citizen --- So I must given up this hope until the time that America becomes more democratic country and stop discriminating orientals.

On one fine moring I went to the store where I work, and found scorched roofs, tables, walls, orange water melons and so force --- Thus I lost my job again. Well, now I don't have to worry about loosing of my job. I am not joking, Bill, this is what I feel.

Sept 19th.

A drop of rain hit me when I came out of library, when I got out of street car it was raining hard. I saw the expression of relief on people's faces. This heat was too much for every body, even for those people who sell soft drinks. We had a shower a week ago and this is the second one since, oh god knows when, may be since early spring. Everything is dry. My life too. There is no sweetness. You saw it in my paintings,, didn't you?

And this is why I read books especially novels. In the book I meet many a friends and their humanness. Tom and the priest in "The Grapes of Wrath', Vincent and Theo in 'The Lust for Life', they touches my heart. It is funny to say, and may be you would not believe it, but while read last twenty pages of The Lust for Life, I could not stop drying. I cryed as hard that for an hour after I finished reading, I felt such calmness that I couldn't think at all. I was thinking up to that time that tears were all dryed up by the bitterness of life. For five years I lived in Los Angeles and yet I do not have even one whom I can call my friend but we are too far apart, and I cann't go back to Seattle on account of my family relation -- although I feel going back to Seattle many a time.

With your and George's, the N.W. Annual should be brighter. Soon I too will be sending better ones. The other day I made a copy in water color after Daumier's oil painting. The result was very satisfactory. I got color as I wanted and it looks as strong as oil! Some one and there are many of them, says that when I paint in water color it should look like a water-color painting! To him I say go to hell! I do not paint water-color painting nor oil paiintings, but I just paint.

Bill: I am very grateful for you kind arrenging my show at so many places; but I don't think it worth to waste your time on them. After all they are mere studies. Of couse if you cash these canvas and water-colors without having show, I wish you'll do it for me, then with that money I can paint more and better one too. Please don't think that I don't care about my paintings or other work. I do care them and keep it with me (at your place or George's is the same thing) if they satisfy me. Take example I like "the desert symphony" now more than at the time I first finished it.

Bill: I should have written you long time ago, but I couldn't, just I didn't know what to say. You know how hard it is to give an advise when I hardly know myself. But I'll write you what think I think which will be best for you.

Judging from you letter I presume that you want painting for your life work; and you are wondering which couse to take as the means of making a living, book designing, illustration or teaching..

I think there are two points in this matter. 1) which one would interest you most, and 2) which one would brings to you surest income. In this case, the later factor is more important, for surest income is the think which makes you to carry out work of your life time. Here I could leave the rest of it up to you. You are the one who must make up your mind.

If you have some reliability of getting a teaching job after some more of schooling, then stick to it, as your family and George says. Then later maybe you can cut down teaching hours if you see good prospects in the field of book designings and illustrations. I know how it is hard to teach, beside all what said and worst of all from our short sightness there are tendencies to discourage real talented young artists. In other words teaching will burden you with more responsibility compared to the others, but it'll give you continuous income and this is the why I, too, recommend it to you.

You book binding and designing are looking your pictures which you sent me, better than average on the market, but I wonder is there enough jobs in it to keep up your living.

One thing I want you to do is to stop the study of the oriental art any farther, unless you want to become a historian! There is no short cut for an artist to reach his destination. You must study from nature by yourself. There is not short cut, Bill. I am afraid of that you are getting to deep in the mud of oriental art; and I afraid of that before you know it the mud be all over you face and you will be looking at the nature through these muds.

Bill, the nature is not same always, as the facts it is changing constantly.

And only those who portray the nature truly become great artist, and those product of artist changes as the nature changes. For example todays Japan is not Japan of Hiroshige, and Hokusai's Japan has gone forever!

I can understand why you are so much attached to the oriental art. The reality or the nature which you see around you is such ugly stuff, full of hatreds, struggle and war. You don't want to see them, it is too much for you. You want to shut your eyes on it, and you want to wander in the dreamland of old oriental arts. But you cnn't and you shouldn't shut your eyes to the reality.

The mere dream and escape from reality bring you nothing but despair and destruction in the end. Instead, you should look into the reality deeper. Bill, don't shut your eyes to stormy sky of today and don't become so desperate. but look up, then you'll see pale but deep calm blue sky beyond the dark clouds; if even the dark clouds cover the whole sky, it you have believe in humanity, then you'll know that there are blue sky -- calm -- beyond the dark clouds.

We, Bill, I certainly did wind up, but this is the way look at the things and the art. One of the reason I sent you "the Guernica" is that Picasso is coming out of the blind alley in which his was wondering since the general cricis of European capitalism that is twenty years ago

All I want to ask you is to stop to give too much of your attention to the oriental art. Would you write me what George is saying on this matter?

After I read this much, I read your previous letter on which you dealt at quite length on the quetion the oriental art.

Well, I am going to pull up my sleeves ans fight to finish on this matter! Now I am going to fight. Watch me!

Bill! I don't like this stuff, called 'Satori'! What is this SATORI any way?. It is a sophisticated way of saying AKIRAME (resignation, abandonment). Satori is the synoym of akirame. You look at it from front then it is satori, you look at it from back then it is akirame, you look at it from an airplane then it is a defeatism, you look at it upside down then it is a escape!

And, oh my god! Satori is not an oriental, you could find in this philosophy of satori in every part of the world (save Soviet Union, for where there is no class, there can not be any grass of satori grow).

No Sir: Satori is not an oriental. Look at the China. Whole population takes up arms and fighting. Look at Japan, the number of stricks are mounting high. Look at India they are waving red flags at the face of British imperialism! No sir, satori is not oriental. You can find it in every place where there exists two or more classes in a community.

The satori was born this way: Once there was an intellectual. He loved peace, but the world in which he live was so full of fight, troubles and hatreds. He disgusted with these things. He made up his mind and went into the no-man-land mountain. He love the quietness. He stayed there. The forest murmuring and whispering brooks teached him a philosophy. This hermit also happen to be a human being and felt lonelyness, so he came back again into the society where people live. He went to a rich man and begged a bowl of rice. The richman fed him for a hermit did not want much any way, and he praised the philosophy for praise cost him nothing.

The richman continued to feed the hermit and let him go around people and preach the newly discovered satori. People said it is wonderful thing. The tenant-farmer, having their new wonderful satori, stoped their complaints (of couse they feared gods too). The hermit still went around. As the result, musicians started to comporse beautiful musics and sounds instead of previouse works which sound like groans of peasants or songs to abuse landowners. Artists, with the magic spell of satori began to paint sacred mountain insteads of miserable people, and writes ----.

(You see long before Marx tell them, the richmen knew that art in a weapon.)

Bill, please don't think I am joking. I am writing seriously, even without going to the evening class.

Then there comes up a question, why so many people think that satori is an oriental philosophy.

Compair to Europe, the orient were not divided into small countries and had longer peaceful periods, and moreover even in the time war the fighting was done by professional soldiers (SAMURAI in Japan) You see, what ruling class wanted from their people was not the fighting spirits, but royality (loyalty) and obedience; They got it by preaching the religion and philosophy of satory instead of force or violence.

You do know that I painted the "Sunflower #1" to express this feeling of satori. then I did not know what satori really is. Nor I had any definate idea of life. That is the why, my paintings at that times varies so much. But since then I think I did understand more. I think I am tired. You see I can not write English to express my thought. I just put down about 1/10 of what I want to tell you. But before I close I should add some more.

Earlier, I wrote that the nature changes. This does not mean a rock become sands or such a matter. When I spoke of the nature, I include everything on the earth including you and I, and whole society. Suppose two people goes to Rainer Mt. and listern to that roaring stream under the glacier echoing whole valley and mountain; one would say, "What might! How small the human beings are!" and the other may feel in that roar the powerful and concistant struggles of human beings for better society.

What brings these different ideas to these two people, though they are seeing same thing? You write that you are tring to understand yourself. Try to understand the organism and set up of society in which you live, then try to understand yourself and your purpose in relation with the society. I think it'll help you to solve your quetion.

The heat is terrable. And this letter went hayfire. I even don't know whether this is understandable or not, any way I am going to bed.

I'll enclose some article from the peoples World. It'll give you clear picture of why in happened and what is happening in Europe to-day.

Yours truly
Shirō

LETTER #54

From Shirō to Bill Gamble

Sept. 30th 1939

Dear Bill:

I was reading your letter of July 16th again. You want to know the name of the "canyon", I don't know it. It does not matter, does it? I spent there two weeks last summer, I mean a year ago. I like the California mountain. Especially the bare mountains near the border of Oregon.

Here I have three paintings. So far the score is that one for me, one for devil and one is unknow for it is yet in the process of painting.

First one is a direct sketch of back yard from my window. Second one is a landscape with a brick house and gasstank I painted this in my room from a small sketch. The third one, I am painting it from my imagination.

"The back yard" I guess the heat got to my head, brush and paints. I hate even to look at. One thing good about this painting is that I did learnd great lessons.

After days of continuous heat waves from the dry desert, there came the storm from ocean. Storm! Storm and rain has magic spell in them. Just as if you washed your face in the morning, the storm and rain brings the spirit of nature to us. I like cloudy day to paint. My best paintings were done in these day. Look at, "The Burn, Winter", 'Up on Yesler', "Georgetown' and 'East Water-way'. I can't understand why Van Gogh went to the south looking for sunlits, just for a simple reason that he painted the sprits or essence of the nature, and not lights. May be he was under the spell of devil impressionism.

Any way, the storm came and I could not quiet down so I went walking in the rain and made a small sketch in water-color. Next day I started for larger water-color from the sketch. It took three days to finish. Meanwhile, the storm had gone and my painting became "after the storm", instead of "storm". This my best painting, so far.

I am not going to send this to you. I want to keep this to myself so I can make it a souvenir to you when George comes. If George does not come then you are not going to see it. You better send George down to get it.

Do you remember I wrote you that I gave up a painting because it is impossible without a model? Thanks for the classes, I can now draw it from my imagination. Yet another difficulties are waiting for me. The color! You can chose any color, but which one!

I am wondering whether I wrote the previous letter too stuborn or too one-sidely.

I am enclosing two press clips which'll not appear in other local papers.

By the way, about a month ago I quit from the Communist party, not because I disagree with them, but I am not fitted to it. So much for today

Yours truly
Shirō Miyazaki

123

LETTER #55

From Shirō to Bill Gamble

Oct 13 '39

Dear Bill:

"Tuscan Spring" a novel about Sandro Botticelli brought me here, that is to San Francisco to see the World Fair.

When I read about the brith of Venus in above-mentioned book, I just could not stop me, so did come. Funny part of this is that when I decided to come here I have nothing but two pennies in my pocket. It was my overcoat, radio and books which made it possible to make this trip. I regret that I sold my bible, Lind Word's Vertigo too.

But the paintings were worth to see them. The birth of Venue was great joy to see. How I wished you could have see it.

To my surprise there were about twelve of the Van Goghs. It was great joy for I never saw his original paintings.

One other purpose of coming here was to see the paintings of America to-day. There were great many paintings with all trend. They were done skillfully. Yet none of them hit me as Van Gogh and Botticelli did to me. Of couse this does not mean that I am going to paint in the style of the two, above mentioned.

Murals were very very good, and "there" were many of them.

Sculpture was poor, so all other things. There were nothing to see in this Fair exception of paintings.

I am not staying with an old friend for one or two days in S.F. then I'll be back to L.A. Meanwhile I'll make some sketches.

Let me know how the N.W. annual is.

I have a new lino-print and a half dozen of monotypes to send to you but I would not send it up to this time for lack of money.

Do you know that the National Art Society with the National Broadcasting Co. is distributing large and good color reprodactions.

Just send $1.00 to

The Art for Your Sake
c/o The National Art Society
30 Broad St.
New York, N.Y.

Then you'll get sixteen of them.

Please give some words to George.

Your truly
Shirō

LETTER #56

From Shirō to Bill Gamble

Oct 19th 1939

Dear Bill:

Your letter of Oct 12th was waiting for me when I came back from San Francisco. I stayed there about five days at the expense of my friend whom I knew when I lived there.

In San Francisco, it was chilly in the evening even I wore sweater and coat; but yet San Francisco warmed my heart up --- friendship. Mistake not, it is not a romance, the friend is male, not female.

Congratulations to you, Bill, passing two paintings at the N.W. Please keep good work.

The rejection of my painting was due. When I saw the exhibition on the Treasure Island, I thought that my paintings are still a child-play. There are long way to go yet. I might add that I did satisfy with the paintings in that exhibition, although there were some which were very close to what I am intended to paint.

In San Francisco, I have had a chance to see a national exhibition of W.P.A. art division. It was a grand show, though infortunatly I could not see the oil and mural division in that show because they were repairing the roof of the museum.

About one third of paintings in water-color division were done with a medium called "gouache". If you know about this medium please give me informations. I want try it out. It seems to me better that water-color for my paintings.

I recieved your letter of Oct 16th with the print, "On Mt. Shuksan". It is powerful print; but it is not power of realism, but a kind of mystery which you name as 'satori'. It is a very very good print

-- this is all I could say now about the print. Maybe I'll write some more after I study it.

I did not start for the painting of sunset. I did not grasp the moods of landscape enough; but I wish I could do it some day for I cannot forget the sunset.

Just as if hungry fish bites the bait knowing that there is a hook in that bait, I took a job.

After I came back from San Francisco, I hardly ate for two days, so there was no alternative course. but to take this job. Now I work in a cafe from 11:30 a.m. to 11 p.m. for $10 a week with meal and only two days off in a month.

What you said about my painting is correct. I tryed in that painting to give each a certain character just as each person in a society have different character, but I failed to unify it as you pointed out. I am painting a street scene with a gasoline station in same technique with the painting, the N.W. rejected. I think I am doing better job this time.

Within a week,, I think I'll be able to send you some of my monotypes and a lino-cut print.

Although, right now it seems it is impossible, I'll try to find out some way, the time and money to attend school for the study of drawing and painting at home.

Please do not try too hard to write me. As far as I am concern it is my pleasure to have some one to write to, especialy a good friend like you and Geo.

With best regard to your Margaret.

Yours truly
Shirō

P.S. Whenever you see George, please tell him what I wrote to you, for I do not write same thing again.

LETTER #57

From Shirō to Bill Gamble

Oct 24, 1939

Dear Bill:

I just came back from the work. My Big Ben says it is 11:30, so it must be. I want to get up early so I can do a monotype before I go to work tomorrow. This is why this letter will be a short one.

I was hungry, that is mentally. Physicaly I am always full now, since I started work in the restrant they force me to eat as much as my stomach bear it, but since then I did not do much reading that is the why I was hungrey mentally. This morning I was thinking to go to the central public library which I pass by every day on my way to work, but when I got to down stair it was no longer necessary to go to the library. I fount your Ozenfants! I started reading the notes on my way to work. It is very interesting. Let me have them for a while   I want to eat them as much as possible. It is very kind of you to let me read them. I will take utmost care of them.

I am wondering is there any possibility to ask Mr. Ozenfant's opinion of, criticisms on my print, the Desert Symphony.

When I showed it to one artist, he said that the composition was terribly bad, as the fact he said "I never knew an artist whose compositions are poor as yours".

When I showed it to another artist, he said the best part of the print is the composition.

Yet, they, both are artist of good standard!

If you could, please ask Mr. Ozenfant what he would say about the print.

Oh I wish I could attend life class!

I thank you for your "Ozenfant".

I'll write again. Please ask George to write to me. I don't care what he writes about.

Yours Truly
Shirō

LETTER #58

From Shirō to Bill Gamble

Nov. 1, 1939

Dear Bill:

Thanks for the Ateliers and the Time. Last night, before I go to sleep I looked over Picasso's drawing and have had a terrible dream all through the night. The recent Picasso's technique is just right for such subject as the Guenica, but people do not feel like that way always. May be I should not say so difinitively without seeing the originals.

I am enclosing "The Background for War" by Gropper. It speaks so plainly why the second imperialist war started this way.

I sent you some monotypes. They are the first ones I have done in this field and they are the all I have done, except one portrait of my friend in S.F. which I sent him.

(1) "Going home, but without job" was from my imagination, I was just like that at that time.

(2) (3) (4) are from my 5 minutes sketches.

(5) a head of negro woman whom I passed by on a street. It was done from my memory.

(6) (7) (8) are, of couse, my self-portrait in San Francisco.

The print was not so successful. I tried to show the strength of labor in rough cut and skillfulness of labor in the engraving technique. I say, I tried!

Since I started work at the cafe, I have not much time to put in my study of art. A monotype a day is the limit. But I'll not make any more monotype for a while because I want to start for a water-color which I promised to the friend in San Francisco who give me food and room during my stay over there.

The Ozenfant note is very interesting, though there are some times I can not agree. For example: he says, "What the average person appreciate? Jazz!" and jump to the conclusion that we must work for such as jazz! If you take daily example, not such abstractive things as art or music, his theory about Jazz is just same to say that the majority of people have old cars or no care therefore we do not need any new type cars!

People likes Jazz. not because it is good music (save that I do not know much about music!) but they are not given circumstances (?) and chances to apreciate good art and music.

When the fifth symphony of Shostakovich was played for the first time last year in Moscow, people (they are labors) went mad and did not quiet down for ten minutes until the composer took a bow. This shoes how the average people can apreciate good music if they live in good circumstances (?) and given chances. In America or in any other capitalistic country a very few people go to the museum, but in Soviet, labors and farmers jam into the musiums, so such as Moscow Musium of Western Arts prohibit entrance of Russian people once a week in order to give chances to the foreign visitors.

Of couse, I agree with Mr. Ozenfant when he says that we should not be a Bohemian, but paint for the people; yet this does not mean we should go after the people and paint cheap picture or make music like jazz. No. We should paint with higher taste with the feeling of majority of people that is toiling masses.

May be I should not start from the disagreeable point to the Ozenfant note, because I agree and learned more from the note than to disagree.

By the way, I remember that I saw a small reproduction of the Bathers #1. long long ago, then I did not remember his name.

I have a clipping which will intresting to you from the People World, you'll find in this letter.

Nov. 2nd

It is 12:30 p.m. now.

I received your letter this morning.

I am glad you saw the exhibition at the S.F. fair. Luck was not with us. If we knew, I could stay over in S.F. a little longer to meet you. Let us hope for other days. Did you like the bare hills on the border of Calif. and Oregon. I like those hills. May be you passed through in the night.

By the way, although I was five days in S.F., I spent only one day at the fair for it cost me $1.00 to visit it and I did not have the money.

Please to not send any more Ateliers. I think I should not read so many various theories in magazine, it gives me only confusions especially when I have not much time.

By now I read through the Ozenfant note. After I take some note from it I'll send it back to you as soon as possible.

There were many things which I did not know and interest me. Especialy his theory on beauty and progression was interesting/

He says we should mix color on palette but in oil painting if you mix color in the canvas then you can get more brighter colors, it is the same theory as the pointillism.

Tomorrow morning I'll go down to the public library and'll brow the Ozenfant book which you recomended to me.

Pardon me my bad English.

This year I got three "not accepted" slips.

This international Exhibition of Lithograph and Wood Engraving is coming to L.A. at the end of the year, so I may have a chance to see what they have which did not get in my print.

How is Seattle? Los Angeles is a crazy town. one day I like to walk in the sun, then next day I prefer shadow. Two days ago it gone up to 99 degree!

I wish I'll be in Seattle and go to painting with you and George together! Adieu.

Yours truly
Shirō

[His address at this time was 648 Stanford, Los Angeles]

LETTER #59

From Shirō to George

Hello George,

I just returned from work, wetted the paper for the watercolor and took a bath. It's after eleven thirty so this letter will be short.

Yesterday, I received a letter from Bill and he mentioned you had all come down for the San Francisco Fair. They advanced the closing date so I thought you might miss it, but it's great to hear that you were able to come.

Your quitting drinking, your coming to San Francisco to see the arts, and then unexpectedly, at the library, seeing your name among the readers of Art Digest magazine. From these, I'm happy to surmise you are returning to your old healthy self.

If you have time, write me your impressions of the art at the fair. Whether you have time or not, write to me. Your impressions on daily life or anything.

It was silly that you went to hear Lily Pons and didn't get to see all of the art. You can hear Pons-san any time. Of course, maybe I say this because I live in Los Angeles. You can listen to Lily Pons every year at Hollywood Bowl in the summer and at the opera in the winter, although I haven't heard her yet.

I hate it when you can't do the things you like and you have to work every day just to eat and to pay back you debts.

I'd like to see your recent works. Snapshots are okay so please send them to me.

I sent Bill several sheets of monotypes and botched block prints. He'll probably bring them your way.

I'd like to learn body drawing, but don't have the chance.

Everything is 'I don't have' and 'it's troublesome'. Eventually, it'll work out. Maybe after the New Year. This year was no good. From the beginning of the year when I accepted that illustration job and wasted time. On top of that, I sent four and three of those were rejected. What a score!

Someday, I'll send the watercolors I have done to the Tsutakawa Museum. It won't be that soon, though.

Go see the motion picture, "Mr. Deed Goes to Town". I haven't seen it yet but it seems to be good.

Go out and buy the novel called "Grapes of Wrath" and read it. I believe it's necessary for those who think of becoming artists to pass their eyes through it.

With this, I put down my pen. I'll write again. Regards to all.

Shirō

November 2nd, night

It must be late autumn in Seattle. San Francisco must have been cold also. Los Angeles is topsy-turvy. The thermometer goes up and down. Until three days ago it read 99 degrees.

[No address or year are given but can be surmised as 1939]

LETTER #60

From Shiro to Bill Gamble

Nov. 16th, 1939

Dear Bill:

I am sorry I did not remember your weding anniversary. I should have sent you my water-color painting to you and Margaret. Well, it too late, so I'll send them all at once, after I get some more.

During last one month, I did not paint at all, though every day I think of going out for sketch in the morning; I over sleep. You see when I come back from work late in the night I cann't go to sleep at once. I read two or three houses. That is the why I cann't get up in the morning. The other day, I read "Conceived in Liberty" by Howard Fast. This is a novel of Valley Forge. I wish you'll read it and know how our country was born. (I am not an American citizen, yet I would like to call America as my country.) Before I read "Man's Hope", I thought I know quite well about civil war in Spain, but the book showed me how little I knew about it; if you read "Conceived in Liberty" you'll feel same about the American revolutionary war. It'll take only one Sunday morning to read through for you.

Now I read "Europe in Limbo" a story of 1914 - 1918. And in same time rereading "Lust for Life".

Since you mentioned "Farewell to Arm" I read it. The material or the subjective matter was very good, but the technique of writing was so poor that I hardly read through. May be better say that the technique of writing progressed so much since the book was published, it looks poor writing for to-days readers.

[This is the end of the letter and not certain if there are subsequent page(s) or not.]

LETTER #61

From Shirō to Bill Gamble

Nov. 21, 1939

Dear Bill:

To-day was, rather yesterday was (for it is after 1 a.m. already), my second day-off. I went to see the international print show. There were etchings and a few lithographs nut no woodcut nor wood-engravings. They did not impress me at all. Of couse many of them came from other countries though. I should say we have better prints in the northwestern show.

I saw twice the California water-color exhibition. There were many good paintings. I learned some water-color tequnich from them. Charles Burchfield's paintings were best.

About gonache: Reading in two books and visit to two artist material stores made me understand what it is. Two weeks from to-day I might be able to buy the colors. Thank you the same.

Bill: tell me about lemon yellow. Why is not a safe color? One of my painting faded considerbly within a short time. May be it was due to panys' grey. Anyway, I look into books including your Ozenfant note, and decided following for my pallet.

White	o	Zinc White - Chinese white for water-color.
Black	o	Ivory or Blue Black
Blue	o	Ultramarine or winsor blue
	o	Cobalt blue
	o	Prussian blue
Green	o	Viridian

Yellow	o	Lemon yellow
	o	Cadmium yellow
	o	Naples yellow (not in tube)
	o	Yellow Ochre
	o	Raw sienna or mar yellow
Brown	o	Burnt sienna or mar brown
	o	Light red
Red	o	Cadmium red or Vermilion
	o	Alizarin madder lake
	o	Madder (garance)

What do you think about above colors? Is there any colors which can be replace Alizrine lake or madder so that I can mix with the earth colors?

I don't know why you like the print I sent last time. What would you say the title will be for the print.

I took some snapshots of my water color paintings to-day. I'll send them in my next letter.

I read now 'the long valley' John Steinbeck's short stories published last year. It is funny that among the art that is music, writing and paintings, I understand, in its technique, writing best; then prints and painting, the music I just feel it without technical understanding.

I started for a painting. I must do some more sketch though. It is a big one. It is like this:

old house

big apt.

hill

bill board

sea of cars

street

(parking lot)

I should not be winding up like this.

Please give to my dear George a big good kick on his pants for he does not write me.

Adios
Shirō

P.S. The letter heads which you made were very good.

[The picture referred to in this letter is his "Bunker Hill"]

Letter #62

From Shirō to Bill Gamble

Dec. 11th, 1939

Dear Bill:

It kept 85(degrees) at noon time every day during November. Now it hardly hit 80. Soon the year will be over. Then winter starts. Snow in Seattle, and dampish weather in Southern California.

Yet I wish the year be over as soon as possible. This year, it was not good year for me. still I am having bad luck. Last week I did not work three days and I do not know about tomorrow for my face has swollen like a balloon and can not go to work for my work is a waiter and no body likes to be served their food by a sick man. I don't know what cause it. Tomorrow I am going to a doctor to find it out. I can not stay out of work too long or likely I'll get canned, though my present employer likes my work, and I can't lose my job right now.

Soft hissing of heater in the corner of my room and gentle foot steps of rain are settings for a quiet evening, but there are, too, hissing of financial troblue in the corner of my head and runing itchy all over my face.

Well I just washed my face with alcohol it stoped itchy, at least for a while.

My painting is progressing at the speed of snail. But it is going where I want to lead it. May be I can send all my paintings and drawings to you and George early next year that is within a month. Last two paintings are very different from others. A word about the snap shot of paintings I promised in previous letters. The camera man turned out to be such a skill man that all film stayed white and printer did not bother to handle it.

I just washed my face with alcohol again.

Do you remember that early this year you wrote me that there'll be an all American artists show in N.Y. which was postponed until next year, and supose to be I am one of those who represent State of Washington? I wonder weather they sent the picture to N.Y. already or not. If not and if still I am one of them, then I like to send the one I am doing now.

Yesterday I finished reading of "The Yearling" by Marjorie Rawlings. It is such a beautiful store that I like recomend it to your wife.

I guess you are busier than the summer bees. Write me after Christmas when you'll have a little more time

Yours
Shirō

Your letter is always wellcome like the sun shine in cold winter day.

Letter #63

From Shirō to Bill Gamble

Dec. 18th, 1939

Dear Bill:

Since then, that is I wrote you last time, I recieved three from you for which I thank you.

I shouldn't have written you about my sick, if I knew that it gives you so much troubles.

My face became normal again, though it itches especialy on my arms and neck and wake me up in the night.

As the cause of this, a doctor told me that it was cause by the poison of germs which got in near by ear. Someone told me it was caused by the cold stomach. I personally suspected, as you did, that it was from negrected tooth. I do not know which one was real cause, for I took care of them at same time. As far as teeth are concerned, I have three or four bad ones. One of them is specially bad. In Japan, a dentist pul out the nerve of the tooth and covered with silver. It silver came off about one and half years ago, so I went to my dentist friend, he started work on it, then he died without finishing it. Since then I did not have any chance to go to the dentist. I'll try to go to dentist as soon as I can in near future.

I did not work five days, but now returned and work, so please do not worry any more.

Last week I read "The moon and six pence" by W. Somerset Maughan published in 1919. It is a story of Paul Gauguin. Tequnich of writing was very, very poor, except the way he built up the climax of the story. Whole book was saved by the climax. I cann't recomend it to you unless you have lot of time which you have not.

Dec. 19th ---

Bill:

I just finished the painting which I started when I do not know but at least one and half month ago. May be I can not say that I did finished the picture, I just do not know what to do with it any further, so I am calling it is finished. The enclosed snap-shot is the place I painted. Please excuse my bad writing, I am tired to-day for last night, after the work in the cafe, I read Thomas Wolfe 'The Web and the Rock' until I heard the morning noise of the street.

The painting I just finished is not so bad, as the fact I feel I am progressing in my painting which gives me a kind weary satisfaction after I put so much in it.

Only the thing gives me worry is that I put a wash with prussian blue over the sea of automobiles in the picture. I am avoiding prussian blue, but I could not think of any other color for it. I was intending to write about the trend which I seek in my painting namely realism, but I am damm tired. I'll listen to symphony through radio and take a shower, go out and have a bite, then go to a movie and will try to rest in the dreamy world of the cinema.

I'll send you my paintings as soon as I get enough money to pack up them Now, I am two weeks behind in my room rent on account of the sick which gave you and me so much troubles.

My regret is that I can not see your paintings. Wouldn't you send me snap-shots of your paintings as you did for your book covers. I don't mean such a good photo but ordinary snap shots. I asked George many times about his but he never send me.

Well, I'll write you again

Shirō

P.S. The other day I bought a frame from a second hand store for your print, Mt.Shuksan. It cost me only 25 cents yet I think it is a best suitable fram for your print. I enclosed a small piece of the back ground, it is a good Japanese style frame.

Preliminary sketch for water color painting,
Bunker Hill. Penciled sketch

[I debated whether to include this drawing, or a gray-tone print of the water color painting here, but decided on the former.]

LETTER #64

From Shirō to Bill Gamble

Dec. 28th, 1939

Dear Bill:

Thanks for you card and the present.

The Webers blocks looks fine, much smoother than the one I used. I thought of prints to make on them. May be set of portraits. But the ambition faded away after looking at your Christmas card. It is a wonder. Especially the omposition! They are getting better every time. After your Christmas card, any attempt of mine will looks like waste of blocks.

Waste or no waste, any way I'll make some prints. This is a good chance to work on small block. I was used to work on large paper in water color and large block in print and almost forgot to to work on small size. In this connection, I notice that your print of a church in Alaska or the Christmas card of this year has the bigness of a good size canvas.

Though it is hard to believe, for weather is warm and winter does not visit us yet, yet within a few days we enter into the new year.

This is the time for most people to look back and look ahead customary. So I too customary yet seariously was looking back and thinking of ahead.

The year I left behind was not any good. I should not waste my time like this.

What I should do in 1940? This is the thing I was thinking and talking with my friend for past several days.

We agreed that first of all we need money. We agreed that we'll go to Sacramento or Stockton at the end of February and work packing asparagus until early May. Then we'll go up to Seattle

(!) and look for the chance to go to Alaska in order to work in cannery. Then by the end of the season we will have at least three hundred dollars each.

My friend needs money badly for his camera and enlarger and so force.

With $300.00, I can settle down, this year I was chase by money all through.

May be I'll settle down in Seattle. Hardly you can guess how I want to be with you and George and study together. May be I'll come down to San Francisco and study the life drawings and mural paintings. San Francisco is the town which has best art school and exhibitions.

Any way with $300 and a part time work, I can go to school, I can pay the tuition. I can buy the materials what ever I need, oil, gouache and water-colors. I can buy the books which I need badly (books were best teacher of mine in print making and painting). May be I can buy even record player and some sets of symphonies!

It isn't bad dreams, Huhm?

Any way, I want go back to Seattle (see how beautifully I can write it name), and want to see you and George and your works!

Seattle, the town of horse chestnuts. It deep color and power. Do you remember the horse chestnuts Van Gogh painted?

My radio say it one a.m. It is the time to sign off this letter

I wish you more works and happier life in 1940.

Your Shirō

P.S. I almost forget: Please ask George to help me in getting chance to go to Alaska cannery this summer. It is a CIO close shop, but I think there'll be some vacancy.

I am sorry retaining your Ozenfant. I'll send them with my paintings in new year.

Thank you again for the Christmas card and the present. I'm sorry i did not do anything.

Shirō

LETTER #65

From Shirō to George

January 1, 1940

Hello George,

Another New Year has arrived. You are probably thinking right now, "This will be the year!"

I hate this thing they call "New Year's resolution". It's because, to me, it seems that the meaning 'when the usual New Year passes, easily forget your resolution' is included in this phrase. Even then, I don't know if it's because of habit, but when the New Year approaches, I get in the mood 'to do this or that in the coming year'.

You probably know since I already wrote to Bill about this, but I plan to go asparagus packing (this is in Northern California) from late February and then, if you would line me up with a job, go to Alaska. I could save up three or four hundred dollars all together if I work one summer. With that, I think I'll begin a student's life at an art school. It looks like this can become a reality.

Either way, I want to return to Seattle once more. I want to also see the streets of Seattle. I want to talk to you and Bill, too although there may be nothing special to talk about.

Actually, I've been worrying about you since you haven't written for such a long time. I know your hatred to write but there hasn't been a single letter since you loaned me the twenty dollars, I'm worried that I might have written something that provoked you.

Even if it's a postcard, won't you send me something now and then?

Tomorrow, I'm sending the pictures I have here by railroad express. Please hold them for me. It's a bother as they're in the way down here. Since you have been keeping my paintings and drawings till now, I'm sending these to be put with those.

I don't have anything special to say, but the painting of the gasoline station indicates the direction I'm heading. A painting I saw at the San Francisco Fair influenced "Bunker Hill"[10]. Years ago, when I was in Seattle, as you know, I never spent more that two days on a single picture, but now it takes more than two months. Looking at "Bunker Hill", I don't know why it took so long.

After finishing "Bunker Hill", being tired from a small illness, I couldn't think about art for two weeks or so, but recently all of sudden, I'm bothered with titles for pictures that keep flashing before my eyes.

Have you read "Grapes of Wrath"? I want to draw this type of realistic art. I'm drawn very much to realism.

Well, I'll excuse myself with this short note. Tell everyone "Happy New Year" from me.

Shirō

[Address not given but believed to be living in Los Angeles.]

---

10 "Bunker Hill" is a watercolor painting (20" x 26") that was done during November and December of 1939.

Letter #66

From Shirō to Bill Gamble

Jan. 3rd, 1940

Hellow Bill:

I just lit a cigarette. It is good. I feel restfulness. To-day is my off-day. I should say to-day was my day for the day is almost gone. I had a good dinner and a hair-cut before I came home. Radio is playing a familiar violin solo. I once had that record but can not recall the name of the tune. No wonder I am getting older, according to Japanese custom we add one year to our age.

But, I am not forgetting to thank you for the lovely letter papers. I was miracle! On that morning on my way to work I was thinking that it will be good to have letter papers with my name on and you will make me beautiful one, but I dismissed that thought for not having money nor a permanent address. Well, at night when I come back from work and opened the door of my room I saw a package on my bed. I opened it. There you are the thing which I wished to have just in the morning. You are such a good friend. I just don't know how to thank you.

Go to George's place whenever you have time and see my paintings. I sent them this morning. There are lots of five minutes sketches and a few paintings. They are all I have done since the fall and I sent them all. I can only guarantee your disappoint especially in the scketchs but you asked for it.

Among the paintings I like "Bunker Hill' best. I tried to put three modes or feelings in, an aristocrat on the hill, suffering masses represented by the mass of automobiles and future. In this you can see what I saw in San Francisco.

In 'the street corner scene' I have had a hard time to balance that big black sign on the wall. These two pictures show the trend I am taking.

This after noon I went to L.A. Museum, and saw a exhibition of two or three hundreds photographs. There was only one I realy liked, and it was picture of bare hills and a farm house with a roof painted with an advertisement of a tonic. Those advertisements and signs in the picture helps lots to bring out the local-color.

I thought to send "Bunker Hill' to the Pacific coast Water Color Exhibition in New York, but gave up. because you and George want to see them, beside I have not money for frame nor the fee.

Since yesterday I was working on a print. The idea for this came to me in 1938. As a fact I was planing to make this as a weding present to you, but finish of the desert symphony delayed and then I was busy with the book illustration and forgot all about it. The other day I found the scketch and decided to work on it. It is rather big one. I am planing to cut on 7" x 16" block, though I don't know whether such big block is on sale or not.

Last night I went to see a French picture 'Marseillaise'. It was a good picture, but there were only ten people attending in whole theater! What a pity! Incidentally director of this picture Jean Renoir is the son of the famous painter Renoir.

That is all for to-day.

Your
Shirō

LETTER #67

From Shirō to George

Hello George,

I just returned home from work. It's past one, but when I read your letter, I want to talk to you about this and that. My head fills up with so many things that even if I went to bed, I probably can't sleep.

It's wonderful you two have started a relationship. It's even better you are seeing each other because you have similar schooling. I imagine that obasan [George's mother] was instrumental in arranging it. I know well what you are thinking, but go out with her with the intention of marriage rather than just as a friend. Of course, there's no necessity to marry right away and hurrying could end up in a failure. If the circumstances for you about her become good, you need to tell her of your intentions. Of course, it doesn't have to be by words. There's that one called 'ishin denshin' [mental telepathy].

Also, always be sure to make time at least once or twice a week to go out together to a movie, concert or play. Go visit her at her home because this is going to affect your entire life.

I'm also happy you're starting to cheer up and want to put all your effort into art, but for me, there is nothing I can say. As an individual, I'm a guy who has no alternative but to go in the direction of art, so I have returned to art. You have much more talent that me to become an artist, but saying that, I can't bring myself to tell you to throw everything into art. However, rotting away your own life for something you don't care for, is something to think about also. You're the only one who can make that decision.

From here, I'm going to continue where I left off the other day.

It's good you went to jail. Now you have the qualification of a modern artist. If you had been beaten up and stepped on by the police like I have, it would be have been better. That's a pity!

Thanks for the money. Guess what I want to buy? I bought two books, "Modern American Paintings" and "Vertigo". To me, I think recent American paintings are superior to European ones. Something is wrong with those who go to Paris these days. Speaking of art, in your letter you only say, "I can see Shiro in his sketches", so I'm thinking that maybe you were disappointed in my watercolor paintings. Of course, that watercolor was not completed, but in "Street Corner"[11] and "Bunker Hill", I think I have clearly shown to some extent the direction I am going from now on. You say, however, that you will critique them in you next letter, so I'm waiting for it. But you being you, I wonder when that will be.

It's wonderful you're doing a mural. I'd certainly like to go back and join you on it. When I save some money and go to school, I intend on studying mural painting. Anyhow, if you're going to paint, paint on canvas. It's easy for the wall to crack right away and it's on a house next to the streetcar tracks. Speaking of murals, did you see in the San Francisco Building at the fair, the mural of a group painted in rhythmical lines of vermilion and black on a white wall. That was so splendid.

Your letter said nothing about Bill. I received these papers, blocks and card for Christmas but not a single line. He must be busy but I'm worried that he might be sick.

I'm beginning to hate this sort of life. All I do is work and sleep. I want to hurry up, get some capital, and work part time so I can

---

11 Which picture he is referring to as "Street Corner" is not clear. There are two large water colors (20" x 26"), one of the Los Angeles Seventh Street Bridge (over the LA River), and another of a gas tank and brick building, both showing street corners.

eat and use my energy toward art. So please go to the union office and ask, so that my friend and I, the two of us, can go to Alaska. Tell them that both of us are union supporters. Whether we can go to Alaska or not, I plan to go to Seattle in late spring. It may be that I can raise only my travel expenses. If so, I'll have to ask you for a bed and meals.

I feel that I cannot settle down unless it's in Seattle. It's only my old man that's a problem.

Currently I'm working on a large 7" x 15" block print[12]. It took over fifteen days to do the draft drawing. Progress is slow because I don't have enough time. On top of that, I've been asked to make a lino cut for the front cover of the San Francisco City League magazine. I need more time, just like you.

Seattle must be cold now so watch yourself. Southern California is warm but I still caught the cold.

Being alone, I'm happiest receiving letters from you and Bill, so write as many as you can. I'm asking you, please.

Please relay my regard to everyone. Until next time.

Shirō

[A date of 1-24-40 is noted on the letter, which was mailed from 648 Stamford Avenue, Los Angeles, California. This address is about six blocks south of Little Tokyo.]

---

12 The large block print referred to in this letter is believed to be his "Kanki no Tsuikyu" (Pursuit of Happiness), which was published in the October 21, 1940 issue of Shisekai Asahi newspaper (Japanese language) of San Francisco in its special memorial edition to Shiro. See Appendix

Letter #68

From Shirō to Bill Gamble

Jan. 24. '40
648 - Stanford Ave.
L.A. Calif.

Hellow Bill:

My radio is playing the From New World Symphony now. I just came back from work and too tired to work in lino-cut which I am working for last three weeks on.

I waited day after day, week after week a letter from you. The lazy George wrote me at last, I tell you it was a joy, but there was no mention about you. Did the devil of illness catch you? May be you are too busy. If you could help, please, please let me hear from you, a short note'll do.

I am tired of this life, work, sleep, work, sleep, work, sleep, worksleep ------ There are so many things to print! Although I know that most of great artists go through these poverty, I am sick tired of it.

Reading between the lines of George's letter, it seems to me that he was disappointed with my paintings. He likes my old paintings which were painted with my heart and hand, but I am leaning that I better trust the gray matter of my head and my eyes than my heart and hand in painting.

The winter up in Seattle must be terrible, though whenever I think of the winter in the north, a pleasant thrill run through me.

I burn heater and wear overcoat, though really I don't need them. We are having good luck this year as far as the weather is concerned, but this monotonous weather makes me idler and makes me to forget that I am going to be thirty by the coming May. Trouble with me is that, like a lazy child, I excuse my idleness saying myself, "There is no need to hurry. Van Gogh started at his thirty! So I can rest until this coming May!! Well?

George sent me money as a Christmas present at middle of January! I bought 'Modern American Painting" and rebought 'Vertigo'.

Many a time I wonder what is life. I read all kind of books, but I never get satisfactly answer. Do not trouble to preach about the religions. Life is hard for me and most of every body, save people or U.S.S.R. May be this is the why you can not fined any joyous colors in the recent painting. I never felt joy nor laughed from my heart for past two, three years.

Write me what you are doing.

LETTER #69

From Shirō to Bill Gamble

Feb. 5th, 1940
648 - Stanford Ave.
L.A. Calif.

Dear Bill:

Today is my off-day. I had none for least three weeks.

I was working on the lino block up to now and tired out myself. I must hurry on the block or else it will miss the train for the coming North-western.

I received your card to-day and a letter previously for which I thank you. Soon you will be a teacher, that sounds pretty good and I bet you'll be a pretty good teacher too, and I hope the day will come pretty soon.

Well, teacher, of couse I am not discouraged by what you and George said about my water-colors, but I was disappointed because you failed to see the big field of new art for which I am heading to. I was used to paint the reflections of mind of mine on landscapes and still-life; then I was just a kid without matured eyes to see the nature, world, society and human beings. No more I paint mere images of my mind but reality.

There are too many of problems I must tackle. One of them is how to paint unified while the reality is full of contradictions. You adviced me to work for sheer beauty of colors and forms. If I do this i'll go back to the old Shiro, the result will be just like the film "Swanee River". Did you see this picture? It is well unified, acting is O.K., colors are beautiful and the musics are wonderful, yet this picture has no life in it. Why? Just because they did not portray the reality of S.C. Forster who starved to death in New York. Oh, it is no use for us, artists, to talk only theories without practice.

Feb. 12th

Since then, that is I wrote previous page, had passed one week. Now I have one off-day every week, then I must work longer hours, 10 hours for 2 days, 12 hours for 2 days and 14 hours for 2 days, so that I could not do anything on the day which I work.

Only the thing I did was reading. I almost finished reading of 'The Eagles Gather" by Taylor Caldwell, the author of "Dynasty of Death". I dare say that his book is greater than 'The Grapes of Wrath'.

I just took the second proof of my print which I began on January 2nd. I think I can finish this print by next day-off, a week from to-day.

Please do not forget that I am waiting for your letter. Always I do hot discussions with you on the problems of art in myself, but when it comes to the time to put down on the paper, it is impossible to do it. I am too slow in writing. Any away you will find me in Seattle on one fine day of early June. I am going to leave Los Angeles early in the next month, then I'll have two or three days vacation in San Francisco, then I'll be packing asparagus some where near Sacramento or Stockton, as I planed on the first day of this year. I hope the things go as I planed, but looks as if I am going to taste the grapes of wrath, or of anguish; Now a days, as a rule, the grapes of labor goes to some body else, but not to the one who worked for.

Well my time is up, Good bye.

Shirō

Letter #70

From Shirō to Bill Gamble

Feb. 19th, 1940
648 - Stanford Ave.
L.A. Calif.

Dear Bill:

I guess you'll be disappointed as I am when you opened the package of print which I am sending to you with this letter. It is just like me, no pitch, no joy and no rhythm. But I know that you are going to send both of my prints --- this one and previous one --- to the Northwestern exhibition anyway; so I enclose one dollar for the fee, and the other dollar will be send to you within one week.

Today, I saw the film "Gone with Wind". It was a wonderful film, very well made. But I don't like the story or content which is a reactionaly one. It says, 'the civilization is gone with wind'; but we can not call the slavery economy as the civilization. Moreover the civil war was not fought in vein, it was a step forward of democracy. Skillfully it side-trucked the sentiment of masses against war into the anti-revolutionary movement. It is wonder that the most reactionary outfit in Hollywood, the M.G.M. spent such a huge amount of money for this film.

By the way, if you have not yet buy 'the modern American painting' as a dividend of the Book-of-the-month club in March though I have one.

I'll let you know three or four days before I leave L.A.

Yours truly
Shirō

LETTER #71

From Shirō to Bill Gamble

Feb. 23rd, 1940

Dear Bill:

You must have been waiting, wondering and worrying for my block print, and by this time, having failed it to reach in time for the exhibition, you must be warming your fist to knock me down. Well I changed my mined. Deliberately, I delayed mailing this letter and package. It, the print, is not worth to trouble to send to the exhibition. This can be said to the previous print too. If I send it early, you'll send it to the show any way. This is the why I held it up to now.

When I started the block, I was enthusiastic enough to make a masterpiece, and during the first month the feelings for the print were enlarged and were mounting higher day by day; but long hours of work for my daily bread prevented the transfer of my ideas and feeling onto the block. After the first month, I just worked on the block mechanically without any inner fire. The result of that is what you saw. I should spend more time!

I am half way on "The star-gazer', a novel on the life of Galileo. It is a great book. By the way, if you have a little bit of time, try to read "Lust for life" by I. Stone. This is a novel of Van Gogh. I think I mentioned this before.

I should have started this letter by thanking for your letter. Please don't try so hard to write to me, though I must confess that if I did not get your letter for two or three weeks, then I start to feel lonely.

I'll leave Los Angeles by March 3rd or 4th. You can send me your letter after that time to

S. Miyazaki
% I. Akiya
1430 Geary St.
San Francisco, Cal.

I must go to sleep though I am not sure whether I have enough will power not to touch the Star-gazer. Last night I read it till 3 a.m. and the day before till 5 a.m. I should get more sleep.

Well, until then,
Shirō

LETTER #72

From Shirō to Bill Gamble

March 8th, 1940

Dear Bill:

Here I am in San Francisco. I got your and George's letters for which I thank you. Yesterday I visited a museum and what do you think I saw there? Your Ozenfant, not him but his paintings including 'Life'. What do I think of them? I don't know. They are paintings which are very far from the world I live in.

By the way what the heck is this? Every time I send you my works of which I am disgusted, you praise them with such big words as 'monumental piece' or 'marveled at'. And you don't think much of it when I send you my masterpiece! The thing that matters in art is the feeling. Extend the hands of your mind. Can you grasp the feelings out of the print? I can"t. Whenever I say feeling, it is not the power or beauty of lines, forms, colors or dark and light, but feeling of our life itself. I thought I could go to Seattle in the near future and talk over these things with you, but it looks like the wind has started to blow against it. If my father is going back to Japan, I think I had better not go back to Seattle, though I wish I could.

March 9th

Tomorrow I'll be heading for the asparagus field where I expect to make some drawings that will become water-color paintings later.

I am waiting for your letter, especially a long one.

I'll write you soon again

Yours
Shirō

LETTER #73

From Shirō to George

Hello George,

Thank for your letter. Couple of days ago, I left Los Angeles and came to San Francisco. That day, I received letters from both of you. I'm sorry I'm always causing you all kinds of worries.

I hear that it looks like they'll be closing a few canneries so there's not much of a chance even if we go. Also, if my father is returning to Japan, although I would like to see him at least once, do you think it would better for me to act as if I didn't know that he returned to Japan? For me to remain here as a student I need money. Even if I asked some commercial company so I can become an international trader, since there are no longer any trade agreements these days, it may be more dangerous to carelessly go to the immigration office.

This was the reason I was waiting. It looks like it's a waste of time to go to Seattle. It can't be helped.

I'm leaving towards Sacramento tomorrow. Even if there's water, they say there is no problem with the asparagus.

Day before yesterday, I saw Ozenfant's exhibit. I'll write a detailed letter after I get there and settle down.

How's your mural coming along?

Regard to all.
Shirō March 9th

[The address was given as 1430 Geary Street, San Francisco, California. Correlating with a letter to Dr. Gamble, it appears that the date is March 9th, 1940.]

LETTER #74

From Shirō to George

Hello George,

I arrived at the camp yesterday and started to work today. I earned forty cents working about two and a half hours. Not being used to the work and there not being enough work, if they take seventy cents for meal, I'll be in the red.

They say a flood hit them so it's no good. Going into April, I think I'll be able to save a little, but if I'm careless, I may not even be able to smoke my Bull Durham. It looks like I won't be able to go to school this year. After I finish here, it's either work in town in San Francisco or near there and if I go for grapes in the fall, I think I can make a little. After I finish here, I might go to Seattle for a week or two. They tell me that the one-way train fare is $13.50, so it's reasonably cheap.

When I was coming here, with the promise that I would return it right away, I borrowed six bucks from a friend in San Francisco for travel and daily necessity expenses. I was going to get some money back from a friend to whom I had lent and who had come here a month earlier, then use that money to send to San Francisco. However, that guy is also in the red because of the meals, so I have only you to ask. Can you send the six dollars to him please? I don't consider you as a money tree but it can't be helped. I'll be able to return it by the time I leave this camp. The party is Ichiro Akitani, 1430 Geary Street, San Francisco, Cal. I'm urgently asking you.

I'll be writing to Bill shortly, but please, let him know my address. I have a little time so I have been pencil sketching. Until next time.

Shirō March 13th

[The year should be 1940. No address is shown]

LETTER #75

From Shirō to Bill Gamble

March 19 '40
RFD Box 163
Clarksburg, Calif.

Hallow Bill:

A week has passed since I came to this camp in Sacramento valley. The life is as simple and plain as this valley. As the result of too little crops and too many workers, we have only two hours work every day. This means that we can not get enough even to pay meals. We expect this situation will continue for ten more days.

What a beautiful dream I wrote you in early January! I am tasting the grapes of wrath now. I'm in such a bad fix that I must give up the bull durham to smork.

Some body mentioned that only the good thing in this country side is that the lundry dries very well. The winds from snow crowned mountains sweeps the plain, so that it is too cold to stay outside, and inside of camp, the air is dirty and stuffy with breath and smork mingled with occasional intestinal gas. My only hope in here is to paint the life in this camp. Up to now I made some drawings and took some color-notes. There is nothing much to write.

How was the print show?

Your
Shirō

Letter #76

From Shirō to George

Hello George,

The rain that pounded down on the tin roof of the shed while we were working today, is still falling on the camp roof, but gentler. I don't know how much longer it will continue or when it will let up.

I'm hoping it doesn't flood. Regardless of whether it's rainy or windy, the Filipinos have to go out to the clayish field and cut the asparagus. We Japs do the packing, so we don't mind the rain but still prefer the nice weather. To begin with, it's cold and I can feel the cold creeping up from my legs. Also I can't go out to do any watercolor sketches.

I have plenty of spare time. Normally, now would be the peak season for asparagus and our working hours should be in the teens; but this year the ground hardened too much with the flood and the weeds grew too high, so they are now plowing up the field with the tractors. We will probably be leaving in about ten days. Today I worked four hours and did just over twenty trays. One tray is 13-1/2 cents, 14 cents or 15 cents. The bosses haven't announced the price. If the bosses quote a low price, the boys won't come. Still they don't want to pay high. So it's the custom not to announce the price until the season is over. If the twenty trays are fourteen cents each, that's $2.80. Since two men worked on it, (one to sort and the other to bundle), it means I earned just $1.40 today. Take out seventy-five cents for meals, which leaves sixty-five cents. This continues every day. Really, it's intolerable.

Thanks for paying my debt. I'm terribly sorry.

According to Bill's postcard, my old man returned to Japan on a ship that left on March 21st. With this, I have become 'The

Outlaw'. If Immigration catches me, we'll see what happens then but I'm not too concerned.

Regard to all. Be sure to write to me.

Shirō

March 27th.

[Address is not given but must be near Sacramento in 1940]

LETTER #77

From Shiro to George

George,

Thanks for the letter. I'm sorry I always cause you so much worry. Especially when the person who's causing all these worries himself, is taking it easy. How do you put up with it? By taking it easy as much as possible, it's feels like I have added some flesh to my face. The way I am now, I don't want to crush that feeling, so I don't want to read my old man's letter. I also feel I know what it says without even reading it. He was born hard headed, so even though he wants to compromise in his heart, he's unable to do it. For you who has been nurtured and grew up among understanding people like your mother and father, it's natural for you to be angry with my father. It's probably best to forget about him. Of course, if you want to lose a little weight, there's probably no better medicine than for you to worry about him. Why don't you read his letter first and if you think I should read it, then send it down.

It really rained. For a week after Easter Sunday, we didn't see the sun even once. Then just when we thought it cleared up for a couple of days and dried the soil, today it's overcast with a sullen sky full of leaden clouds. As for work, although they say work has increased, it's inadequate. Now, if you subtract the loan for the meals and tobacco, nothing is left; however, it should increase from now so that when we leave here at the end of April, I think there will be enough for transportation to the next camp.

You can't make money this way but I'm happy I came here. When I first arrived, I was troubled with loneliness. After eating and working with these people day after day, just like one who can't first see when coming into a dark place after being out in the bright shining sun, I can understand the feeling of those who live a life of destitute. I'm getting to make friends with them. So within the atmosphere of these people, I think I have discovered the mood I had a faint idea of, so recently I am trying to express it in art.

To draw without grasping this sort of a feeling is a waste of time. The life of art after all, is in the feeling to express it. Therefore, the technique should change along with the feeling of trying to express it. When it's said, "Before studying art, become a person", it probably talks about this point.

Often when I awake in the middle of the night, although there are several tens of people sleeping, I don't hear a single snore and it feels like living in a cabin in a virgin forest. Although there are some differences, even during the day, this feeling flows within the camp. Breathing in this air, I feel like playing some musical instrument. A harmonica is too simple. A violin is too large and costs money to begin with. I once played a Japanese Ming flute before and they say that a flute is the easiest to learn. Among the flutes, can you tell me which is the best instrument? My conditions are hard though. It has to be the cheapest, the easiest to learn, has a wide range of sound, is complex and has a clear sound. Do you know whether there's such an instrument that fits all these conditions?

I am happy that with a good pianist and splendid pictures you are painting on your life's canvas. Leave trivial things alone and spend more time with the others. That's what is necessary.

Tell Bill not to worry too much about me.

While listening to the footsteps of the raindrops on the roof, until the next time.

Shirō

April 3rd

[George has noted 4-4-1940. The return address was RFD 163 Clarksburg, California]

See Appendix IV for the letter from our father to Shirō.

Card Players Penciled Sketch

LETTER #78

From Shirō to Bill Gamble

April 14th '40

When I woke up this morning, the eastern sky was burning red and wind was whistling sharp and high; laying on my hay bed, I felt uneasiness, I felt the season's end is near and it is time to go to find another place where I can try to dig the gold.

The nature's phenomenon is hard to foresee, so it cannot be said when this son of the nature will leave this camp or where to go. Any way I'll write you as soon as I reach the next stop in this travel. Meanwhile, if you want write me will you send it to c/o I.Akiya 1430 Geary St. San Francisco, he will send it to me.

April 17th, 1940

What a poor human being am I? I felt joy and pride when I read that they gave an honorable mention to "Pursuit of happiness" in spite of fact that I hate that print.

By the way, I know you are busy but I hope you are painting or making print continuously. For us, artists, learning of theories would not bear much fruits of it unless she lives with a husband, called practice.

Incidentally, it was very good of you placing such a high price for my print, but I too agree with the policy of low prices, it is not a scabing as in the case of working cheap wages.

I thank you for you are doing everything you can for my case. Really I do not know any words how to thank you. I wrote about it to George so by this time you heard from him, so I'll not repeat it here, for I have no time. I must rush this letter.

We may leave here by 20th.

Yours
Shirō

P.S. I read "Native Son" by Richard Wright. It was a greatest novel I ever read.

I missed to send out this morning so I'll write some more.

When I came here about five weeks ago, it was still winter, trees were bare and grasses were young, now grasses are deep in blue, as are trees shining white in the burning sun. In Alaska we saw Spring and summer comes together at once, but here spring did not come at all. You can hardly guess what a great longing I have for your god country where lilac blosoms in purple and horse chest nuts and dog woods in white.

LETTER #79

From Shirō to George

Hello George,

Left the asparagus camp around April 22nd with over fifty dollars. Went to San Francisco for a couple of days and was idle for about three day in Sacramento waiting for work. In the meantime, what I bought were two books (Rodin and a novel), water color paints, lino blocks, sketch book, shoes and a radio ($16.00) and a woman for thirty minutes. With just that, what remained was, can you believe, five dollars in the red? I hated myself.

At this rate, even when the grape season if finished, I question whether I can go to school or not and I'm spurring myself on to resolve to save some money. You tell me, "even cling onto a rock..." I want to do that too, but I wonder.

I started a monkey business. Placing a ladder on a tree, clambering up and tossing down the fruits. Civilized people call this 'thinning'. Thirty cents an hour. Work ten hours from six thirty in the morning to five thirty in the evening and spend a whole day up in a tree isn't bad. When compared to the asparagus camp, it's heaven or paradise.

In front of this camp is a human market. To write more in detail, or in other words, the hoboes wake, live and sleep there without even a tent. So people who need help for lunch come every morning and hire them for the day. If I wanted to sketch this, I can make "An American Landscape".

Writing this far, I started listening to a story about this bogus gambling, so I put aside the letter and went to bed. If I put together all these people's stories into one bundle, it should turn out to be something interesting.

While on a peach tree today, we were talking about closing up shop for a while and go into the mountains, because there is gold in the surrounding mountains. Since we're like the floating clouds blown by the wind, who knows, we may make it a reality.

I plan to stay at this camp for about three weeks. So write to me accordingly. I'll be writing to Bill shortly, but phone him and give him my address.

Shirō

April 30th

[Presumed to be 1940. No address]

LETTER #80

From Shirō to Bill Gamble

P.O. Box 13
Tudor, Calif
May 13, 1940

Dear Bill:

I thank you for your letter which I recieved this afternoon. The letter from friend is a joy on this island far away from civilization.

Yet, it'll be a hard thing to live in a city again after tasting the country air. We are thinning peach trees. We work ten hours every day, six days a week, for thirty cents an hour and we pay seventy cents for meal. Every muscles of our bodies get tired after balancing ourselves for ten hours on the top of twelve steps ladders, but it is not so bad as you might imagine, for it is the pleasant weariness just as you feel swiming and spending all day on the beach, of couse, save the dangerness of falling from the high ladder. Four or five persons fall every day but so far no body was injured yet, yet there is a story that two people died in one season on one ranch.

Well, do not worry, I'll be careful and would not fall. But can not tell. We, people are always optimistic; for example, according to the Fortune survey of public opinion, seventy percent of those who claim themselves are 'middle class' were actually poor! And unless people awake from this optimistic idea there'll be no end for gambling which is so popular among us, because they only remember when they won and they have such a wonderful ability to forget about the time when they loose which is more frequent than gains.

I think I'll stay here about two weeks more, but I say, 'I think", for I cann't tell when I'll be fired. Already, within ten days, more that ten people were fired out of thirty five of us! One out of three!

Last Sunday, I started to cut my self-portrait which I drew last winter on the lino block which you sent for me, well it looked quite different people for my face got lots of fat since then. I guess that this country air is to be blamed for it.

I am tring to make sketches but my pencil is not enough, so I am planing to buy me a camer when this work is over; that means I'll have no money saved for the schooling.

May be I can promise you a large size water-color painting be the time of N.W. show.

Yours
Shirō

LETTER #81

From Shirō to Bill Gamble

May 18th, 1940

Hellow Bill:

The thinning season is over, we are leaving this camp to-morrow. I know not what kind of job is waiting to me, where I am going nor the when.

Tomorrow in Sacramento, I'll start fishing in second-hand stores for a camera. If he starts from ten dollars then I'll start from two, then we'll be sport enough to settle at five.

Now I am listening to a Japanese music through short wave. It program starts 9 p.m. P.S.T. daily, its station JZJ, 11.80 on your dial.

Last Sunday, I tried to paint peach orchard but I found out that I forgot hot to paint. It is a sad thing. If I could save up enough money I'll attend the school from January to May in 1941. This is my plan. God bless on me.

Please call up George and tell him that I am drifting again with winds knowing not where. I'll write you as soon as I settle again.

Yours
Shirō

[Had a Sacramento post mark]

LETTER #82

A letter from Shirō to Bill Gamble

P.O. Box Y.Y.
Delano, Calif.
May 24, 1940

Hellow Bill:

I don't know how the winds were blowing, but I drifted 300 miles to the south from Tudor, and started thinning in grapes wine after I was given a brass button, number 8064 on it, today.

The summer is deeper in this valley, but we could not help it. There was no job for us around Sacramento from where we came and to where we will go back after three weeks of work in this ranch.

In Sacramento I went to "the club", a Chinese gambling house, first time in my life. I went there justifying myself that I should know about these place so that I can write a story; but if I tell you truce, I wanted money so that I could buy a good camera, but in there I lost about five dollars and I have not got a camera yet. It was a good joke on me.

My brain is becoming so plain and simple as this valley and as our life in these camps;, I cann't not write a long interesting letter. I am sorry about it.

Please tell George about my new address.

Yours
Shirō

LETTER #83

From Shirō to George

Hello George,

This morning I awoke with the footsteps of the raindrops pounding on the tin roof over my head. It's cool yet, but if not, it's so hot I can't stand it. When it's lunch and dinner, I'm soaking wet with sweat. Man, what a hot place! They pick only these kind of hot places and plant the fruit trees. The reason given is so that the fruits ripen fast. Do you ask where I am now?

The story goes like this: After the peach thinning was finished, there was no work when I went to Sacramento, so I dropped south some 300 miles to Delano. Thinned some grapes for about two weeks, went back to Sacramento and entered this camp because they said that work would start from Friday of last week. However, the plums haven't ripened yet so I've been loafing around for over a week in this camp. At this rate, if I save some money, it's a wonder.

This camp belongs to a huge company that has somewhere near two to three hundred thousand acres (all of Sutter county). Not only is the company large, the irrigation system is as large as a river. As they have sufficient water, the landscape is very good. The scenery is nice but I have painted only three small watercolors. Being lazy is a problem. Because of this heartlessness, this letter to you is also late.

When I left Sacramento, it was only $1.25 round trip by tram, so I went to San Francisco to see the Fair. The pictures at the art museum had dropped in quality from last year but there were many pictures of modern America so I was able to learn a lot more. It's not worth coming down from Seattle to see them.

When looking at such an exhibit, it makes me want to paint but when I'm painting alone such poor pictures in the country, I feel completely worthless and dark clouds often cross in front of my eyes.

Would you write to me once in a while, too? When I'm in the country, a friend's letter is better than being treated to sushi.

Also, when you see Bill, tell him to read for sure the recently published "How to Read a Book" by Adler.

Until next time. My regards to everyone.

Watch your health, too.

Shirō
June 19th

LETTER #84

From Shirō to Bill Gamble

July 7th, 1940

My Dear Bill:

I have been on the bank by a river. It was the climax of the day. Sky was in blue of strong summer and clouds were in red of golden brightness. I stood there watching to-day's departure. How beautiful was it, I cann't tell, except to recall the passage, "Music, when soft voices die, vibrate in the memory-----."

When I watch the passing of time I become sentimental and when I think back of past and of to-day I sank deep into regrects. I have done almost nothing. After finishing thinning of peach at Tudo on May 18th, I stayed at Sacramento until May 22 when I went 300 miles south to work only a little over two weeks that is until June 7th. Back again to Sacramento to wait for a job. On June 12th, I went to a camp at Sutter Bashin and stayed there for two weeks and worked only 46 1/2 hours! On June 16th back again to the capitol and July 1st I came in this camp and already to-day in July 7th still I am waiting the work to start. You see, last month I worked only 46 1/2 hours and recieved a big amount of $4.10. There is no wonder that I am so deep in red that is about $18.00.

There would be no regrect, had I spent all these spare time usefuly. But I did nothing to speak of except a few small paintings. As far as the paintings is concerned, it is partly due to my lazyness and partly the circumstances of constant change of localities, that is that there are not enough time to grasp the feelings of each local.

Incidentally, speaking of paintings, about a month ago I have been at the San Francisco Fair too see the new exhibition. I was glad I went there. There were many American painting of new trends.

I cann't tell you whose paintings they were, for my memory is not so bright and I did not have enough money to buy the catalogue. I learned lots from them. By the way there were two Burchfield, every time I see him his painting is new to me.

Now the piccaso's are in San Francisco, but too bad I can't go to see them.

I did not tell you yet where am I. I am on a delta of the Sacramento river about thirty miles south of the capitol. Our camp locate midest of pear orchards along the river, But most attract me here is the white clouds against background of deep and strong ultramarine.

If you are teaching now I recomend you a book called "How to read a book" by Adler, a professor at Chicago University on this subject for fifteen years.

By the way I am anxiously waiting for your long letter which you started from last year.

Please give my best regards to Margaret and George.

Yours,

Shirō

P.S. Please send all mails to c/o I. Akiya 1460 Geary St. San Francisco, Calif.

Letter #85

From Shirō to Bill Gamble

Aug. 4, 1940

Hellow Bill:

Working I am, and eat and sleep. I do feel healther now a days. If the money is coming in a little more, then there'll be no complaints I can make. We get up so early in the morning that when I go to walk to peach orchard a couple of stars and if I sarch more carefully I could see several more of them shining in the dark blue of the Hiroshige. We stop the picking of peach at 3 p.m. then until 7 o'clock I work with a young man putting in several thousands of empty boxes for the next days picking. Hard work it is, at least for me. I am not builted for this kind of work. Yet there is glad I am. I am feeling fine though awfully tired I am.

Your letter was forwarded from S.F. just in time, I received it in the morning when we left the camp. And the 'Tempo' a day before to it. You are kind to me. I don't know how to say. I am a lucky guy, I should say having fellows like you and George as my friends. How many others have as I have, I do wonder. George does not write to me much, but I know he is thinking of me and worring about me.

The Memorial Day 1940, your print, was a bit of surprise and a big pleasure to me; at it was great stimulus for my lazy mind. The composition, I take my hat off. Different technique were mastered very well. There is a little lack of refineness. I guessed that it was due to lack of time, and you letter told me so.

I wish I could got back to our city, Seattle But. This is a big but, for two reasons. For one, I don't think there is any life class to attend for the other I am so poor that it hardly keep sole and body together, it I take example in my shoes. To San Francisco, I'll go. But, here is too another but, only when I have enough money to pay fee for school and a enough money to live until I can find a after-school job.

The ten dollars, I am glad to fine in the mail. This is the first one from the sale of my art work. $10.00. When will the next one come? May be years after. I wish I could buy something to remember by with this money, but I am send the check to pay back my debt.

Did you read 'Native Son'? This is a book you must read wether you have time or not. I just finished the reading of 'How green was my valley'. I read it slowly so I can taste it better just as we eat good meal. I enjoyed this novel though a little reactionaly in its content.

I have no painting to send for the fall show. If you mind, I wish you to send the water-colors of parking lots. I know you don't think much of it but there is not any others either.

By the way do you know who is this Mrs. Lloyd E. Jensen who bought my print. I am wondering why that kind print while there are many of great names. I must close this now.

til next time good-bye.

Shirō

LETTER #86

From Shirō to Bill Gamble

Acampo, Cal.
Sept. 16.

Dear Bill:

Please lend me a piece of you brain. I am in a bad fix. When there is the alien bill on one hand and the draft on the other, a man of my age should have a permit or a card of one or the other, I guess. Is there any possibility of escaping it? Should I go to a post-office to give my figure print? What shall I do? Please write your oppinion. It is a troublesome time.

Whether Wendell Willkie or F.D.R. there will be no mistake predicting that America will enter into the robbers war after the election. They can not miss this golden chances to grab the spoils of war as they did in the World War No. 1. Are you planning to make a print of the Christmas 1940 after 'the Memorial day, 1940'?

How are you now-a-days? Are you teaching in any school? Or still in the university?

I am in a camp of a grapes ranch. By the end of October I think I can clear a little over $100.00. After this, I am wondering whether I should work two more months and go to the art school in January in San Francisco, or should I go to Seattle and have some talk with you and George. I am so lonely that I need some encouragement from both of you. But if I go up to Seattle I'll use up all my money and there'll be no schooling. Really I don't need any schooling, but the art school is the cheapest way to do the life drawing, and more over I feel that I need some training in the field of sculpture so that I can hold of feeling of mass and power.

I wished to write you a cheerful letter, but may be due to the cloudy sky or may be due to the cup of beer I had last night, even the piano from my radio sounds dull.

Please give my best regard to your Margaret.

Yours truly
Shirō Miyazaki
Shirō

[This apparently is the last letter from Shirō to Dr. Gamble.]

LETTER #87

From Shirō to George

Hello George,

It's been a while. I haven't heard from you for a long time, but what are you doing? Did you draw a picture for the autumn exhibit?

I've been going here and there under the big blue sky of California. This time, from four days ago, I've been picking grapes. I'm working with sulfur, used as insecticide, and the sweat mixing to give me a good tan. Still, it a good-feeling type of work. Here the work continues from now until the beginning of November, so I'll probably have enough left for tuition to go to art school this winter. To be doing this is really stupid. Even working at one camp for two or three weeks, your pocket is empty before you know it if you go to town. No matter what, money never sticks to me. Next time I go to town in a month, (it'll work out somehow, although I really don't have any expectation), I intend to put all the money toward art. To write a little more in detail, with the grape and following with celery will provide for tuition from January to May plus one month's living expense, so if I can find an after school job in a month, I can go to school until May. At school, I intend to take up life and sculpturing. I have to take up sculpturing because I am still weak in grasping a three-dimensional feeling. After I finish school in May, I think I would like to find a half-day job and devote the other half toward art.

The other day, I drew on a lino block so it's ready for cutting. It's a picture of on a California highway, with Oklahoma migrant workers as the theme. I'll cut it later after I go to San Francisco and settle down. By the way, sent me some snapshots of you works. I want to know what kind of art you are drawing.

Rural California has many things that can be used as subject for art but I can't go walking around camp with a large sheet of paper and mainly I can't compose myself. Someday I would like to paint the rural landscape. Still I don't think I can paint it through the eyes of a farmer. That's because I still don't fully understand the farmer's feelings. I'm a laborer through and through. I read this kind of thought in a novel of Van Gogh's life, "Lust for Life" by Stone.

Living a camp life, I long for friends I can talk intimately with and for a concert hall. I yearn to listen to the gloomy music of Beethoven's Third Symphony. In camp, you can't play the radio loud enough, because they all go to bed early.

How's your girl friend? Why don't you hurry and get married. I think it's better that way.

Tomorrow is Sunday, but there's work so I'm going to sleep from now.

My regards to everyone over there. Send me a letter!

Shirō

Next Time Try the Train (8-1/2" x 11-1/2")
This is the linoleum block Shirō refers to in Letter #87.

He never started cutting it and this photograph is the unfinished block.

The picture is penned in India ink. Note where all the wordings are in reverse.

Where Highways US 50 and US 99 intersect as shown in the picture is located in Sacramento, California.

Water Tower at Volunteer Park Seattle
(Linoleum Block Print (8" x 10")

LETTER #88

From Shirō to George

Hello George,

Unexpectedly, I went to the San Francisco Fair for the art exhibit because it will close on the 29th of this month. I went because I wanted to see Botticelli's "Birth of Venus" and also wanted to know the direction American art is leaning toward in general. Even if there was nothing else to see at this fair, I wasn't disappointed.

The European art from the 15th century to the present was expertly arranged. Among them were more than twelve Van Gogh's, so I felt that it was a bargain because I had never seen a Van Gogh original. He is good. There is not one unnecessary touch.

There were hundreds of pictures by American artists. Various techniques were used and the exhibit was very educational. Kenneth Callahan's "The Blind March" was there too, but none of them swayed and firmly grabbed me the way Van Gogh did. I wasn't very impressed with the selection.

Only the pictures that were painted in the gloomy ateliers received awards. The realism that shines under the sun of this American continent, this realism that shows the ruts of American capitalism, does it shine so brightly that it blinds the eyes of the judges? Even though they were far better than those that won awards, they received none.

Among the close to a thousand paintings, I didn't see a single watercolor. Yet from the oil paintings, I was able to learn watercolor techniques. I will probably start painting again in oil one of these days.

There were many bound books like those done by Bill. They were all luxuriously magnificent and made with thick leather and shiny gold. I think it is regrettable that bookbinders don't try more to artistically bind ordinary inexpensive books.

Murals are the ones to see at the Fair. The concept I had of murals was quite different from what were there. The murals were decorative but the coloration was such that no matter how long you looked, you never tired of looking and were terrific.

This trip was a cheap one costing me $7 for travel, $1 for fair admission and $1 for food for a total of $9.00. I was planning to just see the Fair for only a day and return right away to Los Angeles, but my old friend told me to enjoy myself, so I decided to stay for a couple of more days. Yesterday, I went to see a mural at Recreation Park made by the WPA. Then I walked the waterfront and did some sketching.

When I return to Los Angeles, I'm planning to make some monotypes. Monotype is really fun. Have you ever tried it? For some reason or another, I decided I wanted to try it, so a few days ago, I started in the evening. It was so fun, I continued until late into the night. Using the brown ink for block printing and an oil paint brush, you paint a picture on a sheet of glass. By varying the strength and the direction of the stroke, an interesting light and shade pattern is made. On that you etch white lines with a pointed stick as you would with block printing. Then you rub it with Japanese paper. It's best to use a wax pencil when you make the first outline on the glass.

I plan to return to Los Angeles tomorrow. Until next time.

Shirō

[No date or address is provided although it's clear from the letter that it was written in San Francisco. George had noted on the letter Sept. 1940.]

LETTER #89

From Shirō to George

George, thanks for your letter.

I hear you're sick too. I presume you're well by the time letter reaches you. I'm sick too and spent the last two days in the hospital. The illness is asthma and happened about two weeks after I started work at this vineyard. Two nights ago around midnight, it suddenly worsened to where my throat got blocked so I couldn't breathe and I was wandering in and out between consciousness and unconsciousness. My boss brought me to the hospital and after a shot I felt relief.

I'm planning to leave the hospital, pack up my things at the camp and leave for San Francisco. There's no worry any longer.

The worry is, I don't have much money and whether I can find work right away or not.

I am happy to hear you are earnestly into art.

Details will be sent later. Notify Bill of my going to San Francisco too.

Until then.

Shirō

[No date or address is provided. This is believed to be Shirō 's last letter as he died on October 7th, 1940.]

POSTSCRIPT

While working on this book, I wondered what I could find of my brother in the internet so I looked him up on Google. There was only one website, Ask Art The Artists' Bluebook – Worldwide Edition. It was noted " Shiro Miyazaki is primarily known as <u>Shiro Miyasaki</u>". In Chinese characters, Miyasaki and Miyazaki are the same and pronouncing it either way is correct; however, in the family register, it can be only one way and in our family, it is Miyazaki. His one paragraph biography contained several errors, stating his birth date as January 1, 1912, that he immigrated to the United States in 1927 and that he died of tuberculosis.

Since this book could be published only in black and white or gray-tone, it was not possible to include any of Shirō's art that were in color. Depending on how this book is received, I am considering the possibility of putting together another book with all of his artworks I have. This would include his water color paintings. linoleum block prints and etching, along with pages from three of his sketch books I have in which he drew in preparation of his finished art.

Appendix I

A Will of Hideo Miyazaki (our father) written to our mother prior to his departure to America in 1915. (Original in Japanese.)

WILL

At this time, I am leaving my aged parents and most beloved wife and child behind and am crossing to foreign borders. As this is my one great decision, you should be aware of this. That is, it is satisfactory even if a portion of my goal is not rewarded and although I may be stricken with illness, or fall into a dangerous situation and end up becoming a part of North America, I am determined not to return to Japan. While there is no one but God, who knows of life or death in advance, and as I am but a human who cannot measure morning or evening, I wish at this time to relay to you who is my wife, my desires as my Will. Also matters left behind and entrusted to you are not unnecessary. This is the reason I have recognized the necessity of this document. Therefore I have separated the sections and listed them below.

1. If a person's happiness or unhappiness is to be determined by a length of time of five or ten years, think of today's misfortune as the first step to another day's happiness and hereafter never be discouraged or anguished by unexpected hardships, but always fight with courage. If you encounter an extreme difficult situation, you must be prepared to exert your greatest courage to overcome it. Especially the future of the Shimamoto family is a piece of puzzle so do not look into the future from now. In addition, with an undercurrent now in the family, there are always a never ending trickery and small troubles, so while being alert, let it not bother you and stay calm.

   Man lives with hope. Because a hopeful man thinks of the future, he does not mind hardship and therefore, courage rises by itself. I earnestly wish you will seek happiness in the future and live with hope.

2. Since whether a person is healthy or not is the dividing point of his fortune or misfortune,. Always take care of your health and, furthermore, when you recognize anything that is detrimental to your health, get rid of it by all means so it doesn't happen again.

   Since the action of the spirit has a great effect on health, always stay cheerful, refreshing and cool. If you should become ill, collect the courage of your entire body, fight the illness and never surrender to the illness. Rather than pity and lament over your own self, I hope you will recognize that there must be ways to overcome it.

3. I need not mention that virtue is a woman's life. Even if this should not be true, if there are any scandalous rumors, it will have the same result as one without virtue. There are many in this world, women whose husbands are away who have fallen into the abyss of forsaken love by deceitful acts of those with skillful persuasions. Especially, since there are many who want to say, "There is smoke even though there is no fire", you must avoid at all cost, getting in a situation where people can question, nor approach a questionable person or a man you have met only once.

   I absolutely believe that while you lead the life of a lonely wife, your conduct will be prudent and discreet. Yet it will be for a long time, so I leave you these words of precaution as one cannot say that such an occurrence will never happen.

4. Change your indecisive actions and be active. Correct your leaving things half-done and become orderly. You must improve your mind of many superstitions to one that is most civilized. This is the way to improve yourself and also is most important and necessary for Shirō's education.

5. For the next several years, I will struggle with all my might and set up a basis for living and plan to call you and Shirō as soon as possible, so get in that frame of mind from now. The final happiness of man is harmony in the home, so I wish that the three of us can make an ideal home in the paradise of North America. From ancient times, it is a principle that a woman follows her husband when she marries. If you have the will to help me in my endeavor, think of me and have the zeal to think of Shirō's future. I believe that you have the determination to go to a foreign country and live with me.

Therefore, in order that you will not be reluctant to leave your mother and hesitate later in going to America, you must be prepared from now. Care of your mother will take care of itself.

6. You should know that in the future, I plan to return to the Miyazaki clan together with you and Shirō. Furthermore, secede from the Miyazaki clan and manage an independent household. This is your brother's, Yoshinosuke, real intended desire and I too, wish this for our future's sake.

7. In the event that I should die, whether you should remarry or not, I leave to the wishes of you and your relatives and have no objection. However, in the event Shirō stays with you, with regard to the family register, he is to be my successor.

8. In the above event, take Shirō with you to Tsubaki-domari [Tokushima prefecture] and take care of matters by consulting with the Miyazaki clan relatives. At the same time, although it's a small matter, I have entrusted some of my clothing in Tomari, so take them all as a keepsake for Shirō. Furthermore, there is a satchel (a Chinese satchel) that I left in Tomari where I could put my personal belongings. Although there is no monetary value, take all of it and use it as reference for Shirō. In there are two packages of papers wrapped up in Japanese paper. You may keep them or burn them if you have no need.

Shirō's culture is of the utmost importance, so I will write in detail. The final happiness or unhappiness of a human being all rest on one's child. Namely, it must be said that the wisdom or folly of a child is determined by whether the child is healthy or not. Especially with Shirō being our only descendant born between us, whether we have happiness or not after we become old, depends on how Shirō turns out. So now, it is your sole responsibility to see that Shirō is brought up healthy; both in spirit and body. Although I cannot stand to see you bear this great responsibility alone, as the children get influenced and education mainly from the mother even if we were living together, the greater portion of child education is your burden. To date, however, many times, your method for Shirō has been with favoritism. This is not necessarily always your fault, but comes from the deficiencies in your home. That is, you were brought up with your mother's blind love from the time you were very young and had your way with everything. Because you had your way, you do not have the ability to penetrate and discern a person's mind. Therefore, many times, your attitude toward Shirō is inconsistent. Of course, this type of self-training will require great effort and the first step in educating Shirō is to know yourself along with your self-training.

The following are the details:

1. Pay attention to health
   a. If a person is healthy, even though he is uneducated, he will be able to make a livelihood. Other than learning and education, health is anyone's most important requirement.
   b. The first harm to health is in the dietary system from eating and drinking. When the gastroenteric system is weak, it affects the entire body, especially with young children, so you must be moderate with the food. Urging a large meal on a child is the same as urging him to get sick. Once when you urged Shirō to eat a lot, I was alarmed and could not bear it. Many times, people get sick from over eating but never for eating a small meal. I wish you to thoroughly consider this reasoning. Especially limit eating between meals and don't let him eat to his heart's content.
   c. Clad him in as light a clothing as possible and let his skin toughen.
   d. Once he becomes ill, you must have a doctor examine him and treat him. Do not feel constrained by the family and hesitate in calling a doctor. The reason an illness becomes critical is because treatment was neglected at an early stage.
   e. On the other hand, however, giving medicine without cause when there is nothing wrong with him will weaken the system, so appropriate thought must be given.
   f. He should be awakened early as possible in the morning and limit the evening to around eight or nine o'clock and put to bed. Especially, allowing a young child to stay up as late as he wishes will have a bad effect on his mind.
   g. Teach him to be courageous and let him exercise. To foster courage is the first step to health.

2. Intellectual education should be taught gradually and must never be abandoned because you are too busy or your dislike. Education should never be left solely to the kindergarten school.

a. Intellectual education must be complete. Going just half-way only tires the child's brain.
b. When he learns and comprehends writing, let him write compositions. When he studies mathematics, make him apply it to other subjects.
c. From now on, people without a mathematical mind will be the loser. Rather than let Shirō develop in the direction of literature, you should endeavor to make him excel in the direction of mathematics and take measures for Shirō's interest to be always in mathematics.
d. When he returns from school, as long as he does not become sick, always make him study for twenty of thirty minutes under your supervision. Improve his skill with reverse study, by questioning him on what he learned that day.
e. There is a saying that it is not good to reproach a child; however, that is a matter of degree. But to think that education is complete at school is an extreme case of not thinking. Do not mind comments of others but make your own decision on what you believe.

3. Do not forget for one day to exercise the mind and spirit.
a. The education from now on must be education with a purpose. Blind love will not bring good results for the future. At times, you must reprimand and reproach him with appropriate consequences. However, to constantly scold and reproach a child, results in the child despising the mother, so this must be refrained. In other words, when you must scold, really scold him and gain your objective without minding the mediation of others. Always have love deep in your heart, however, for scolding in anger doesn't have a bit of effect.
b. At bedtime, going over the events of the day together, comment of all the things Shirō did, fully explaining what was good and what was bad, is very effective.
c. Keep your movements brisk, exercise discipline, make him do what you directed and be sure you do not stop in the middle.
d. Strong intentions mean strong disposition. Strengthen Shirō's disposition and do not change him to be timid.
e. Make him remember that his father has gone to a far distant place and that he retains his love and attachment for his father. This has a great effect on discipline.

f. There is no necessity to educate him together with others in the household. They are they and we are we. There is absolutely no need to copy what others do, but gradually discipline in the direction you believe.

Although the above outlines the training for (1) physical development, (2) intellectual development and (3) spiritual development, education is a living thing. Therefore, when you recognize something that is good, act according to the circumstance. What I have written above is my aim in Shiro's education and cultural refinement from now on, so you should follow this as a guideline. In other words, it will be sufficient if you work toward Shiro's healthy body, his cultural education, intellectual training appropriate for his age, and to strengthen his willpower. Over-sensitiveness without reason toward Shiro is detrimental in building a great man.

Especially for the training to strengthen his will, you must first improve your own willpower so as to be like steel. If the teacher is weak willed, it is impossible to strengthen the willpower of the pupil. To reach you objective, there is no need to fear people's criticisms and comments. I especially repeatedly warn you of those around you who regard it their mission to criticize. Toward them, take an absolute superior attitude and do not alter your planned steps for Shiro's culture because of criticism.

POSTSCRIPT

1. The above, which I have disclosed with sincerity, are the understandings along with my desires I entrust to you while I am away. If unfortunately, I should die in between, this will become my Will so keep it in safe place.

2. In times of hardship and distress, I hope you will always use this and that it will comfort and encourage you.

3. Don't neglect to write to me from time to time. For one who is far way, even a piece of letter is a comfort, so write from your side even if you receive none from me. Not to write because you don't receive one from me is imprudent. Be mindful of it in the future. As we will be far apart, write in detail as much as possible of what is happenings, your thoughts, Shiro's and your health conditions, changes and development in Shirō's body and spirit. Also include photographs of yourself and Shiro from time to time as well as his report card, etc.

4. If at times, you do not feel well, don't feel constraint by family members and rest. Also cut down on your sewing.

That is all.
May 26th, 1914
Hideo Shimamoto
To Kuniko

[Note: Father signed it Shimamoto (mother's maiden name) because he was adopted as my maternal grandmother's son (yōshi) and his name was transferred from his brother's family registry to his mother-in-law's registry when he married our mother. Later he established his own registry under his former surname of Miyazaki.

APPENDIX *II*

A telegram from Kōno of Osaka Mainichi newspaper to Hideo Miyazaki

WESTERN UNION

1929 MAY 25 AM 3 31

FB79 RCA= F OSAKA 31/29 25 343P
LCO MIYAZAKI   TRY MIYASAKI AND CO
SEATTLEWASH=   952 24 AVE SOUTH

KIKANO   REISOKUWO   HONSHA   TOKUHAINNO
KAZOKUDE ARUTO SHOMEI SUREBA NYUKOKU DEKIRU
RASHIIGA SOSUREBA SHORAI KIKAGA HONSHATONO
KANKEIKIRETABAAI ZENKAZOKU NIPPONE HIKIAGE
NEBANARANUKOTONINARU   IKANI   TORIHAKARU
BEKIYA=OSAKAMAINICHI KONO

IF NOT FOR YOU PLEASE RETURN BY MESSENGER

[Translation of Telegram]

It appears that if we certify that your son is a dependent of our company's special correspondent, he can enter the country; however, if you do that, in the event your association with the company is severed, your entire family will have to return to Japan. How shall we handle it?

Kōno of Osaka Mainichi Newspaper

[This is how Shirō, who was born in Japan, was able to circumvent the 1924 immigration law prohibiting admission of Japanese nationals for immigration purposes. Traders, diplomat, newspaper correspondents and their families were allowed to enter. This was the sword of Damocles hanging over his head when our father left for Japan on March 21st, 1940. Of course, the portion stating that the entire family would have to return to Japan is incorrect in that my sister and I were born in Seattle and were therefore US citizens although we were minors at the time.]

APPENDIX III

史郎より父への手紙　　一九三七年六月十一日

ロス・アンゼルスより

お父さん

御別れしてから二日目の朝無事に羅府に着きました。御安心ください。汽車の旅でつかれたのと一寸忙しかったので御知らせするのがおくれました。こちらの気候はシアトルの此の頃と同じ位ですから身体にはこたえる様なことはありません。今仕事口をさがしています。一二週間の中にはみつかることと思います。

今の所まだはっきりきまりまっせんがうまく行けばそしておとうさんさへよければ来年位にシアトルに帰れるなるだろうと思ってゐます。お母さんを失った後だし潤子や脩作がオレゴンへ夏休みに行ってしまへば後はすい分さみしいでせうが元気にゐて下さい。これから時折お知らせします。今日はこれで失礼します。僕からも手紙を手紙を出しますけれど皆様によろしく云っておいて下さい。では御身を大切に。

再伸。吉見さんのミセスがあの金を知らぬ間に蔦川さんから貰って来た紙袋のなかに入ってありました。折角ああして下さるのだからいただいておきます。史郎

　　註　　史郎が渡米以来親に書をよせたるはこれが初めてのそして

　　　　　最後であった。母死して多少心境の変化を来たしたるもの

　　　　　とみえる。この書は母の四十九日忌を済して再び加州に去

　　　　　りたる直後のものである。末文「あの金」云云は史郎が去

　　　　　るに当り吉見が餞別として贈って来たのだが可成り大金で

　　　　　あったので余が辞退したものであった。それを史郎の友人

ジョージ蔦川に託して彼が封筒に入れて別れる際それとな
く史郎に渡すよう計ったものといえる。

Letter from Shirō to father from Los Angeles dated June 11, 1937

Dear Father,

The morning of the second day after we parted, I arrived safely in Los Angeles so please do not worry. I am late in notifying you as I was fatigued from the trip and also a little busy. As the climate here is similar to that of Seattle in this season, it has not affected me. I am presently looking for a job and think I will find one in a week or two.

Although it is not clear yet, it appears that around next year, if it is alright with you, I think I will be able to return to Seattle. Since mother passed away and after Jiunko and Shūsaku goes away to Oregon during their summer vacation, you must be very lonely but please stay well and healthy. I will also try to keep you posted. I will end this letter for now. Please take care.

Postscript: I received an envelope from George Tsutakawa unknowingly that it contained that money from Mrs. Yoshimi. Since I received it in that manner, I will accept it.

Shiro

Father's Note: This the first and last time that Shirō has ever sent me a letter since he arrived in the U.S. It appears there is a slight change in attitude since his mother's death. This letter was written after his mother's 49th day memorial service and had returned to California. In the latter part of the letter. "That money" he refers to, when Shirō was leaving, Yoshimi came with a quite large amount of money as a farewell gift that I refused to accept. Therefore, it can be said that Yoshimi put the money in a envelope and asked George Tsutakawa to hand it to Shirō as they were saying farewell.

APPENDIX *IV*

From Hideo Miyazaki (father) to Shirō

On my returning to Japan on the March 21st steamer, I will recognize this one letter.

Since I am leaving this America soil forever, I thought of allowing you to say farewell to your brother and sister. However, although both Jiunko and Shūsaku speak of their dead mother, they have not once said "niisan' [older brother] since you left three years ago. Also it was because I was afraid on the assumption that you might hit your juvenile younger brother again, they may look down on their 'older brother' in contempt forever. Shūsaku is now fifteen and over five feet two inches tall, has joined the boy scouts and has become stronger than you, so I'm afraid that if you two get into a fight, I won't be able to stop it. However, they both listen to their father's orders, enjoy studying and are keeping up to have a healthy body so on that point, don't worry.

There is one thing I want to leave with you in parting. You proclaimed to me once, "Father, I thought you were a greater man, but really you are petty". So be it that from your view point, I may be 'petty'; but I think I did a man's work, although it was only trivial. Let me list the undertakings of that petty person. Leaving my wife and child, I came to America when I was twenty-eight. For travel expenses, I borrowed a hundred yen from my father and two hundred yen from my older brother. On top of that, I started working from the day after I landed and within five months, returned all that I had borrowed.

Helping with the living expenses of wife and child back in my native land, I sent tuition for the eldest child, Shirō. In the sixth year, I started an export business without any capital. And again, I became an insurance agent and a newspaper correspondent until today.

Whether I grow thin and wither away, for the past twenty-five years, economically, I have never bothered my parents nor siblings, let alone other people for even one cent. Not to bother anyone to be sure, on top of supporting wife and children, I sent twenty-five hundred yen as tuition for the eldest son in Japan. Two thousand yen in the past ten years to my brother for helping care for my eldest son, and several thousand to my aging parents till their deaths, to repay for but one ten thousandth of the blessings they bestowed upon me. Why I am poor today is no coincidence. Even though poor, as a parent to a child and as a child to a parent, as a husband, as a brother, I have done these things. So even though you scorn me as being petty, I am satisfied in my heart. As a parent with a thirty-year old son, I should be in a position to be able to retire; however, because I have such a splendid eldest son who would insult his parent, I must still continue to work.

Let me ask, you who speak ill of your father. It is eleven years since you came to America and are now past thirty years of age. What kind of business or work have you accomplished? Reviling your parent, slighting your benevolent grandparents, aunts and uncles, forgetting your respected teachers, if you're as highly a person as you judge yourself, you should be a great man by now.

Jumping into a labor movement that your parent opposed and burning your hand at the end, it's good that you returned to art, but aren't you ashamed by just drawing pictures with your clever hands? If you know what shame is, you should reflect upon yourself, discipline yourself and study.

Also remember the following conditions as my Will:
1. I name Shūsaku as my heir. (Therefore, there is no need for you to provide support to your parent, brother or sister. At the same time, do not ask for help from your parent, brother or sister.)
2. Although you never requested it, I submitted the papers for your draft deferment every year till now, but I won't be able to do it by law after I return to Japan so take care of it yourself. However, if you plan never to return to Japan, you may do as you like.
3. In Seattle, although they may not say anything, they know that while you were in Seattle, you laid your hands on me. If you come

to Seattle, there is no one but George Tsutakawa to greet you, so don't come back to Seattle to shame yourself.

4. When you came to America, you entered as a member of my family, so when I return to Japan, you are in a position where you should return also. Be prudent and try not to put yourself in a position where the law can find fault with you. There are many in Seattle who knows this. Since there is the risk of someone informing on you, don't go to Seattle.

Living in America for twenty-five years, separated from my wife by death, defied by my eldest son, with disappointment, I give thanks by leaving this country forever.

I pray for your health.

Father
To Shirō

Notes:
1. This letter was written in 1940 just prior to our departure to Japan.
2. The incident where Shirō hit his brother (me) happened in May 1937 when he returned to Seattle to attend our mother's funeral and I was eleven years old. We were arguing who was going to listen to what program on the radio. He wanted to listen to a symphony while I wanted to listen to some other program such as Gang Buster, I don't remember which. He slapped me and I was crying when our father happened to come home. If I had been wiser or could have known the consequences, I probably would have gladly let him have his way.]

APPENDIX V

Letter in Japanese from Hideo Miyazaki (Shirō's father) to George

Please excuse the informality,

I received the telegram from Mr.Yoshimi and was astonished by the unexpected sudden death of Shirō. I don't know how to express my thanks for your going to California on my behalf. On top of your helping him whenever he asked for something, I'm very sorry you were made to look after the final arrangements. Please resign yourself as having the misfortune to have made a good for nothing like him as a friend.

The telegram only said 'died' but what was the cause of death? I am imagining various things, such as, in the past he hurt himself quite badly when he wouldn't listen to me and bought a car, so was it a car accident, or was he ill? Or did he commit suicide because of a disappointed love affair, despite his being hard headed and one with inadequate feelings?

Although he was constantly disobedient toward his parents, it is pitiful when it comes to this and I feel so sorry for him. However, I have lost a wife overnight in the past and know very well that nothing is certain in life, so I believe that everything is destiny. Returning to Japan, I found out that Shirō had a bad reputation among his relatives. But that is no wonder because in the ten years since he went to America, he has not once written to any of the benefactors who looked after him, or those who loved him. Therefore I am planning to keep it a secret from the relatives for a while. There is no one other than myself who feel truly sorry for his death.

I sent a wire to Yoshimi-kun to take care of everything for the time being and not to hold a funeral. I asked him to have his ashes forwarded here. Since he was single and as I am not in Seattle, it is not right to have my friends and acquaintances hold a funeral for him. Actually to hold a funeral cost quite a bit of money, so

I don't like to trouble them to pay for it. So if his ashes are sent here, I think I will have the funeral here and bury his ashes with his mother. After consulting with Mr. Yoshimi, please forward his ashes when you have the opportunity.

During my twenty-five years in America, I experienced arranging funeral services for eight or nine of my bachelor friends. It is a lot of trouble. When I think that people are taking care of the affairs after death of my own son, I am deeply moved. Even then, for you to go to far away California to do it, I thank you again and again.

I believe you had travel expenses to California and other expenses, such as funeral and cremation, that you had spend, I have wired Mr. Yoshimi for him to repay you so please accept it.

Please relay my regards to your two uncles, Hiroshi[?] and Joji.

[Last sentence not translated.]

October 10th at Tōkyō
Hideo Miyazaki
To Jōji Tsutakawa

I doubt there were any of his property kept in particular, but if there are any, after consulting with Mr. Yoshimi, please dispose of them in any way you please. Should there be at least one of his paintings left, if you could send just one at you convenience as a keepsake for Shūsaku, it would be appreciated.

APPENDIX VI

An article in the Shinsekai Asahi Shimbun (The New World Morning Sun Newspaper) A Japanese newspaper published in San Francisco. Monday October 21, 1940 edition (Original in Japanese)

PURGATORY SYMPHONY
(Offered to the Soul of Shirō Miyazaki)

By Ichiro Kariya

The moment the moaning of suffering stilled, the heart beat suddenly stopped. My nerves numbed and it felt as if my whole body was being steadily pulled down to the bottom of the deep sea. When I felt like I am in a syncopic state, a sharp inner consciousness reflectively started to open my eyes. "Hey, Shirō", I weakly called. With eyes half open and leaning on both of his arms, there was no breath of life in him. The steam heater rattled as I looked at my wrist watch. The small hand was pointing to 3 AM. October 7th, 1940. "Shirō, have you really gone to sleep, forever?" but he did not move. He, who feared death, no longer looked like he did. I closed my eyes tight and remember our past friendship.

Shirō Miyazaki died young. I am full of emotion, to where I want to let the pen write for itself but my brain is too sentimental for it. Shirō was a guy who threw his young life into literature, art, block prints and struggle for bare existence. What was he thinking recently? What was he dreaming? Let him tell you himself. The following are excerpts from his diary:

January 1, 1938

Feelings on inactivity I'm looking through a collection of the Imperial Academy art exhibition. Groups and groups of nude figures, landscape after landscape. How long am I going to draw these? The clock continues to tick away. I'm sinking away not being able to have a girl friend.

May 18th

Chase them away, chase them away and still they come back. Hungry are the mosquitoes of the hills and plains. The water that flows between the plowed rows like a large river. Drink it and grow fat, you tomatoes.

July 6th

(Dream) Ah, it finally arrived. Without work now, how am I going to pay it? It can't be helped, take it away. But won't you take that car for twenty five bucks? Because while I'm at it, I want to take care of the hospital expenses. My shoulders feel light like summer clothing. Take the car. What did you say? I owe you twenty five bucks? Oh, so it was, so it was. I awaken.

December 2nd

Borrowing a book on drawing at the library, when I came to the corner of Fifth Street and H, I discovered a statue of Beethoven that I had never noticed before, or rather I must have looked at it with attention today. It's just like me. The button of the vest is missing and the face is etched with the melancholy lines of hunger. So it's not unreasonable that we both have no tie with women. In the corner of this small park surrounded by tall buildings of financial capital, he silently stands in the shade, day after day, year after year, listening to the footsteps of the people of the time whose heads are full of emptiness. The bright sun shines in the park just as it shone in the Vienna Woods when he wrote the Third Symphony. Even though time has passed from the beginning of capitalism to its collapse, he continues to watch the sufferings of the same people from this corner of California. While walking in the park and thinking thus, I thought I would write a poem, a poem called "Statue of Beethoven". So I returned to the library and borrowed his biography. I found out later that it was written by Roman Roland.

December 5th

Poetry is gone from within me. To dig out the dormant poetic instinct is most important now for me to proceed in art.

December 6th

While listening to Tschaikovsky, I realized that there is no feeling in the print of the astronomical observatory. When I finish the Desert Mountain, I'll start on it. Besides these, here are some themes I would like to work on:

1. The mass of workers exiting from a factory gate. The evening sun casts long shadows on the ground.
2. The main theme is marriage where the man is leaping toward the sky. The woman is also leaping and helping.
3. A life size self-portrait.

December 20th

As I finished about two third of the desert scene block print, I printed the upper half and hung it on the wall. It's not bad! It's not bad! I'll title it "Desert Symphony". All I have to do is to cut the desert portion, but therein lies the problem. What sort of music shall I put in it? That's the problem.

December 28th

The world makes much ado about Christmas. I worked very busily. And that too passed by. Every year, it's the same. Alone. I decided against the title "Desert Symphony". "Naked Nature" or just "Desert" is better.

January 1st, 1939

Sitting on my bed and playing around with the corn on my foot, the factory horn started to blow. It is now 1939. Although it's a holiday, probably the night workers are blowing it in self-abandonment. It's a long one, continuing for ten minutes.

January 18th

The poetic instinct is fading again. I want passion.

January 20th

Drawing a HIP BONE, I was surprised at how rhythmical it is. It's indeed a large symphony. (Note: On January 8th, he met a bacteriologist Berl ben Meyr of Silver Lake through Heihachi Kamiyama of Los Angeles and contracted to do the illustrations for a book "Your Own True Self". Miyazaki spent over four months painstakingly finishing several dozen illustrations and casually left Los Angeles. Then when the book was published in

August, ben Meyr and Kamiyama searched for Shirō but to no avail. When they hear of his death, the book was presented as an offering to his departed soul. I wish to report that Miyazaki's great mark in art is plentifully included in this one book and also recommend your reading of same. Akiyama)

April 3rd

A letter from the Seattle Art Museum that was included in a letter from B, stated that they sent one of my paintings to the National Exhibition of American Art (New York) as an representative of Washington State artists. Why does E and also T belittle my art? To begin with, they don't recognize me as an artist. I wonder why. Is it professional jealousy? It can't be just that. On the other hand, those in Seattle hold me too high. To reach there required a lot more study.

September 29th

The burning heat from the desert continued for a week. Then an unusually warm wind blew in from the ocean. The sky is covered with a penny gray color and everything on earth has been washed in the rain and have bared their individuality like baptized souls. I couldn't stand it any longer, so splashingly walking in the rain, I made a small sketch of a gas tank. But while I was painting in my room, the storm left and the gentle autumn sun started to shine. Then the painting changed from " ---- in the Storm" to " ---- after the Storm".

August 7th

In addition I must get the car overhauled. This will cost fifteen dollars. I'll have to pay at least six dollars for the radiator and right bumper. I need close to a hundred dollars. My torn shoes, shirt, socks. When I think of it, there are more things that require money than the dust in my room. I want to buy wood for my block prints and if I go to art school, I'll have to pay tuition. Then I want to buy records and a record player. Goddamn money. Money, money.

September 29th

I never dreamt that to draw a picture from imagination was so difficult. To begin with, a sheet for a draft of a nude. Another sheet for a draft with a fully clothed figure. The third for a complete picture in black and white and the last for the distribution of the

213

colors. Altogether four sheets for draft are needed. To imagine and compose with color is not a simple task. Just for the flesh tone, there's red, blue, green, so it's very difficult.

October 3rd

I dreamt I was fighting. Why don't I see more peaceful dreams? In one form or another, the enemy appears in my dreams.

October 11th

In my pocket are a dollar bill, one nickel and three pennies. What a headache. A cheap cigarette and empty stomach. . . .

October 17th

My leg hurts. My stomach is empty. Encouraged with a bottle of Coca Cola, I went to the art museum. The museum that I had heard as the desert within the Worlds Fair, was full of people. I can't settle down to see the paintings. Among the old Italian paintings, the "Birth of Venus" was the best. A Cezanne and twelve Van Gogh were an unexpected piece of luck. Van Gogh's shone through all of the rest. Those in the American group were all good but something was lacking. It's probably because the ordinary life of a worker in general was not there. The winners of awards were a pitiful lot.

October 19th

This morning when I arrived in Los Angeles, I had sixty seven cents in my pocket, but I spent fifteen cents for hot cakes, laundry twenty cents, library two cents, buttermilk five cents, and five cents for Durham which leaves me with only twenty cents. Amen.

APPENDIX VII

A column in the Shinsekai Asahi Shimbun (The New World Morning Sun Newspaper)

A Japanese newspaper published in San Francisco.

Monday October 21, 1940 edition (Original in Japanese)

SUBURBAN LINE
By Kominami

The man who submitted novels and poems under the pen name Shikichi Hara, his real name was Shirō Miyazaki. Early morning of October 7, the 15th year of Showa, he completed his life on this earth. On October 9th, officiated by missionary Reverend Nagatomi, the funeral service was held at Martin & Brown Funeral Home in San Francisco. Among the more than fifty people whom attended, a third of them were Americans whom I hear were all his friends. Besides George Tsutakawa of Seattle and Ichirō Akiya of San Francisco who handled the funeral arrangements, Heihachi Kamiyama of Los Angeles and Terumitsu Kano of Seattle provided great help. I also give thanks to the other sympathizers.

Apparently there were many who enjoyed Shirō's linoleum cuts in the literature column of Kashū Mainichi newspaper [Japanese newspaper published in Los Angeles] and the literary magazine 'Shūkaku' and rightly so, for he was acclaimed quite highly among those in the art of block printing.

The illustration 'Tree of Life' in the book 'Your Own True Story' is wonderfully made and his friends talking among themselves, say there is nothing to be ashamed of in the text by the one who introduces "the Japanese artist, Shirō Miyazaki".

The large block print 'Pursuit of Happiness' shown on this page had a price of twenty-five dollars at the exhibition. Someone said he wanted a print but couldn't afford the twenty five dollars so he asked if he could have it for ten dollars, It is said that as this is someone who understands art, he was given it at that price. This was not the original block but just a copy from it.

[The remaining portions of this column has been omitted except for the post script.]

Post Script

Most of the page of this edition has been devoted to Shirō Miyazaki with writings by two or three along with Shirō's prints to express our sorrow.

The large print 'Pursuit of Happiness" and the two smaller prints were added to fully fill out the page. The 'Pursuit of Happiness' has received good reviews from among the Americans.

Pursuit of Happiness
(15-1/2" x 8")

This picture of the block print was photocopied from the Shinsekai newspaper.

APPENDIX *VIII*

An inset in the Shinsekai Asahi Shimbun (New World Morning Sun Newspaper)
A Japanese newspaper published in San Francisco.
Monday October 21, 1940 edition

TO SHIRŌ MIYAZAKI
By Kazuo Sumie

An angel of the "SUNFLOWER'

A public square of rock, grass and flower

One lonely star begins to shine.

APPENDIX IX

From Karl Ichirō Kariya to George

Tsutakawa-kun,

How have you been since I saw you last? As you took a week's leave, you must be busy since your return to Seattle. How is Bill doing? Have you received the copy of the Shinsekai Nippo newspaper's memorial edition of Miyazaki-kun I sent you? I edited it in such a hurry, it didn't turn out satisfactorily. The Kashu Mainichi newspaper in Los Angeles also favored us by publishing a memorial edition. If you wish a copy, I think they will send you one if you request it.

I received about fifteen dollars from his friends in Southern California as 'kohden' [monetary offerings]. I was expecting more, but as they hear of Miyazaki's death, the kohden is gradually starting to come in from out in the country. One came from New York. In the near future, I'll have to cut it off. Then I want to arrange the Kohden List and forward it to you.

I think you were anxiously waiting for the autopsy report from the coroner's office. (I was the same), but yesterday I finally read the coroner's report. (My wife made an appearance at the coroner's office with Dr. Kitagawa.) When I read the report, I was surprised at the unexpected result. What Shirō and we believed to be the cause of his illness was not asthma, but was identified as lympho-sarcoma of the lungs (commonly called 'zahcomu' in Japan), that is worse than cancer. This sarcoma develops very rapidly and is said to be a fatal malignancy. A hundred out of a hundred who get this do not survive. Although it's too late, I regret that we paid $18.00 to the Lodi Hospital that diagnosed it as asthma. I couldn't even laugh at the hilarity of Shirō taking the asthma medication to try to stop this illness even if I tried, for the asthma he thought he had and we had accepted the diagnosis. There were no indications of asthma, heart problems or epilepsy. The sarcoma developed in the windpipe and appears that it reached an asphyxiating condition very fast and sudden. Remembering Shirō who died in extreme agony at the end, it's too late to stop shedding tears. Let us pray for the repose of his soul.

Are you proceeding with the block print work you took back there? I would like to see it soon, if possible. As you are so busy, I hope you do it when you have the spare time.

Shirō 's free diary that was addressed to you was lent to some of my friends who wanted to read it, so please don't think ill of me for being late. I'll send it as soon as possible.

I haven't heard any more from the funeral home so I have left it at that. (As I was able to get Shirō 's money, everything was paid up in the end.)

Yoneda-kun, husband and wife, Saitō-kun, Kaida-kun (he is in Sacramento now but will return to San Francisco soon) and Hayakawa-kun (he is farming in Mountain View but must be sad as he considered Shirō as his only friend) are all well. My wife is well also, however, ever since Shirō's death, I've been a little out of sort and am taking care of myself. She asked me to give you her regards. In the near future, I would like to go see where you are.

The matsutake mushrooms were very delicious. I divided them and gave some to my younger sister and Yoneda-kun. They were very happy.

As it is going to get colder from now on, please take care of your health. Also give my regard to Bill.

I want to also put Shirō's letters in order and although it bothers me, I can't get around to it. I plan to do it gradually.

The contents of this letter are topsy-turvy, so please use your own judgment. I'll write again. When you have the time, please let me know how things are up there. Until then.

From Ichirō Kariya

Note:
1. This letter was in Japanese. George had noted on the letter, 'S.F. Shiro's friend'.
2. Kun is similar to Mr. or Miss and is usually used between those of similar stature, and used mostly between males.
3. I found out in 1999 that Mr. Kariya and his wife took the responsibility of caring for my brother during his last illness and also his funeral. Mr. Kariya died in 2001.]